Straightening the Crooked Horse

Gabriele Rachen-Schöneich
and
Klaus Schöneich

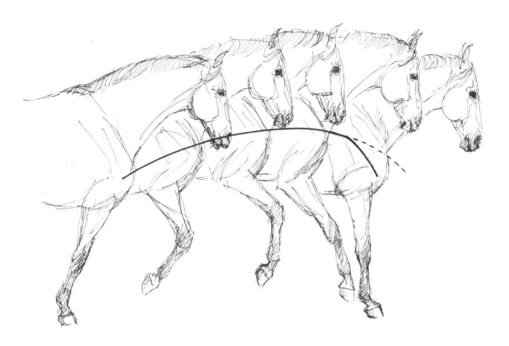

Straightening the Crooked Horse

Correct Imbalance, Relieve Strain, and Encourage
Free Movement with an Innovative System
of Straightness Training

Translated by Chris Belton

Trafalgar Square Books

North Pomfret, Vermont

First published in the United States of America in 2007 by
Trafalgar Square Books
North Pomfret, Vermont 05053

Printed in China

Originally published in the German language as *Die Schiefen-Therapie*® by Müller Rüschlikon Verlag, Postfach 103743, 70032 Stuttgart.

Library of Congress Cataloging-in-Publication Data

Rachen-Schoneich, Gabriele.
 [Die Schiefen-Therapie. English]
 Straightening the crooked horse : correct imbalance, relieve strain, and encourage free movement with an innovative system of straightness training / Gabriele Rachen-Schoneich and Klaus Schoneich.
     p. cm.
 Includes bibliographical references and index.
 ISBN 978-1-57076-376-2 (alk. paper)
 1. Horses—Training. 2. Horses—Diseases—Alternative treatment. 3. Horses—Physiology. I. Schoneich, Klaus. II. Title.
 SF287.R33 2007
 636.1'08967—dc22
                         2007013841

ISBN: 978-1-57076-376-2

Cover design by Heather Mansfield
Book design by Sabine Heüveldop

Illustration credits:
Photos courtesy of authors, except pp. 146–7 by Ricarda Bausch. Drawings by Renate Blank.

10 9 8 7 6 5 4 3 2 1

Contents

The Diagnosis

Correcting Crookedness: Practical Work

6

Six Testimonials

Acknowledgments

We are convinced, above all, that veterinary practitioners, trainers, and others responsible for dealing with the horse's problems, need to accept that crookedness is a cause of many of them.

We should like to take this opportunity to thank all the horse owners who have entrusted their horses to us. Without them we would not have been able to accumulate the knowledge that we are now passing on through this book. Though it is impossible to mention everyone by name, we would also like to thank all those who stand, or have stood, steadfastly by us.

However, there is one name we should like to mention. Much of the work involved in the preparation of this book could only be done successfully in an atmosphere of peace and quiet. A special word of thanks is due to the Hotel Voss in Westerstede for providing this.

Preface

The need for an explanation and information about the horse's natural inborn crookedness and heaviness in front has never been greater. It is a topical theme, as shown by increasingly frequent discussions on the subject. We cannot help but be surprised that so many horse owners, trainers, saddlers, farriers and even vets are unaware of strain on the horse and dramatic problems in its way of going that are caused by uncorrected crookedness. It is for this reason that we have brought together in this book our experiences with more than 4,000 horses over a period of many years. *Schiefen-Therapie®* (Straightening the Crooked Horse) follows on from, and expands on our previous book *Anatomisch Richtiges Reiten* (Anatomically Correct Horsemanship). Since the publication of that book in 1999, so many important developments have taken place that it was obvious a new book on the subject was required.

 Gabriele Rachen-Schöneich

The first question, obviously, is "What is our system for correcting crookedness, and straightness training?" Let us explain what we do. For over 25 years we have been intensively involved with crookedness in horses and its effects. It became increasingly clear to us that this difficult subject had to be seen as part of the "big picture" and that we needed to take an integrated—meaning holistic or "whole"—approach to it. We realized that the horse's heaviness in front, together with its crookedness, affected it both physically and mentally. This meant experts in different fields would be required, and that they would need to work together on the project. To tackle all the aspects of this difficult problem, we realized that we needed to establish a base where we could work with all these different experts together.

 Klaus Schöneich

This is how we came to set up the *Zentrum für anatomisch richtiges Reiten (ARR®)* (Center for Anatomically Correct Horsemanship). This may seem like an odd or even confusing name as it could give the impression that we are teaching a new system of horsemanship. We chose this name quite early on when we first started working on the project and were trying to make clear that if the horse is not moving freely it is working incorrectly from an anatomical point of view. If the problem is tackled and overcome, the horse's way of going then becomes "anatomically correct." We thought, and still think, that this is completely logical. Following on from this, we then asked ourselves: what do we have to do to achieve this anatomically correct way of going? We came to concentrate on one area in particular, namely crookedness and heaviness on the forehand. Hence we became specialists in this field. We are in no doubt whatsoever that not enough attention is paid during training to making the horse straight. This means that there is a big gap in the training.

We see it as our job to close this gap. The aim is the same, whatever the breed or the purpose for which the horse is used. While the horse is with us, we try to work closely with its regular rider. We explain, for example, what we are doing with the horse and how we think the training should proceed after the horse returns home.

As part of the corrective process, we also talk things over with the horse's veterinary practitioner and farrier to ensure that all aspects of the problem are addressed.

Unfortunately, we often come up against opposition from veterinary practitioners, which we find difficult to understand. For example, at many conferences, long discussions take place

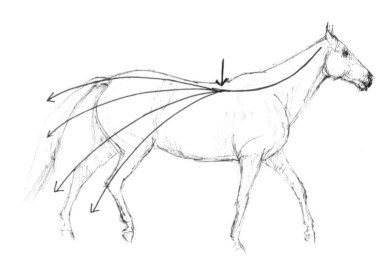

● *How the horse moves naturally.*

about ways to treat back problems in horses, and while this is a good thing in itself, we hope that this book will lead to even more research being done into the causes because in our experience, these back problems are often the result of uncorrected crookedness.

We have written this book especially for riders—be they competitive or pleasure—and for everyone who is passionate about riding. It should serve to provoke thought and discussion, and also answer a few questions. However, it also has another purpose, which is to make everyone who deals with horses aware of his responsibility. Every trainer, rider or horse owner must understand his horse's needs, and then ensure that it is treated and looked after accordingly.

Over the years, we have worked with many horses. These horses came to us as a consequence of incorrect or insufficient basic training, bad riding, wrong veterinary diagnoses, incorrect management, and faulty or incorrect saddlery and equipment. With our system of straightness training, we have successfully treated the most diverse problems displayed by modern-day riding horses, and returned these horses to their riders cured.

We have found that all too often horse trainers fail to consider the developments that have taken place in horse breeding over the last 50 years. Today's sport horse has extremely power-

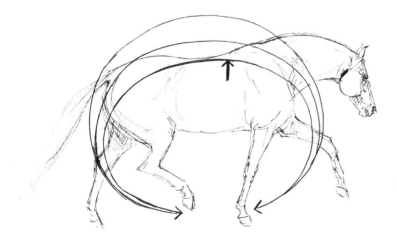

The correctly trained horse working through its back with rhythm and impulsion.

THE BIGGEST DIFFERENCE

What is the biggest difference between the horse's anatomy and that of man? The following simple comparison shows the main distinction:

Man is *vertical*

Horse is *horizontal*

ful hindquarters, and problems inevitably arise if the rider fails to take this into account when training. It is our job to make sure that he understands the origins of the crookedness, knows how to recognize it, and above all what to do about it.

We believe that about 95 percent of all problems in the horse's action and way of going are caused by its intrinsic crookedness and the effect this has, for example, on its locomotive system if the crookedness is not corrected. It is important that riders and trainers understand this, and it is our job to explain it so they do. We demonstrate how to identify problems and correct them. The first part of our task is the diagnosis and from the outset, experts in different fields are involved so that the problem can be treated as a whole.

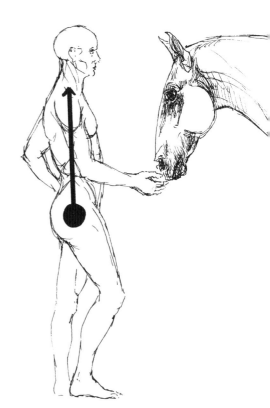

◀ *The main anatomical difference between man and the horse: man stands upright and the horse is horizontal.*

The rider can only carry on successfully with our system after returning home if he has understood how to work with the horse. We, of course, give practical advice on how to do this.

We actually believe that young horses should be given straightness training even *before* they are backed. This prevents them "wearing out" prematurely. So, we have therefore included a section on working young, unbroken horses, as well as problem horses from the ground (see p. 66). The transition from work on the ground to work under saddle is also explained in detail (see p. 83). Finally, there is a section containing case histories written by the riders of successfully treated horses. They show that no matter how serious the problem, there is always a solution.

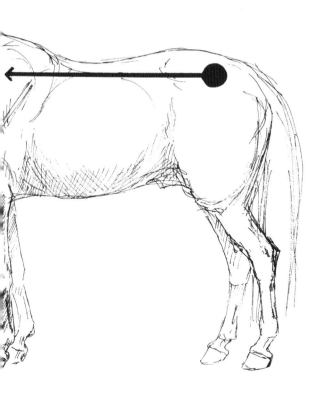

Introduction

MOTION PROBLEMS AND CAUSES

This is the start of a voyage of discovery, during which you'll need to be prepared to make several detours. You need to look at the basic principles of riding from a different angle, though still accept them in themselves. Though the subject matter is familiar to most, this journey is not for everyone since we go to a level where some readers may find it difficult to follow.

In its natural state, the horse carries more weight on its fore-hand than its hindquarters, and this forward center of gravity combined with natural crookedness has far-reaching effects on its training, health and soundness, and leads to seemingly inexplicable problems related to its way of going.

Before looking at the individual aspects, let us make clear that all the points we will be making in this book are based solely on our own observations and practice. They are the results of the work we have done over the years with horses, owners, trainers and riders.

All statistics quoted are our own, based on our experience over many years. From our records we can say with certainty that a good 95 percent of the horses that have visited us have been affected by significant motion-related problems and tension. A large proportion of these problems could not be fully explained by veterinary medicine. However, through a positive collaboration between vets, farriers, trainers and owners, and appropriate straightness training on the longe, these horses could usually be brought back "on track" so they could go on to develop their performance capability.

We place great importance on this longeing training. We firmly believe that a horse needs thorough preparation before it is ridden. Our priorities in this training are straightness, strengthening the "carrying" elements, that is, the musculature, and getting the horse to take more of the weight of its trunk and forehand onto its hindquarters so that it is no longer heavy in front.

We start with the assumption that the horse is by nature, heavy in front as well as crooked. We accept that every horse is made this way and is affected, although to a different degree.

These two conditions cannot be ignored and, if not corrected, will have a very negative effect on the horse's health and soundness.

At this point, we must caution you against a tendency to just focus on the horse's symptoms and veterinary and other treatments at the expense of proper training and hard work, which happens all too often in our experience.

"Crookedness" is a term that keeps cropping up in horse training, but its importance is often underestimated. Once you become involved with it more closely, you'll realize how important it is, and finally, how easy it is to understand. It requires, first of all, careful study both of yourself and the horse.

The simpler it is, the harder it seems.

What we hear most of all from the riders who bring their horses to us is: "I understand crookedness in theory, but have problems putting it into practice." The problem is that man stands upright, that is vertically. You need to put yourself in the horse's place and "think horizontal." This is quite complicated. You need to find a way to simplify the process, so a few fundamental issues need to be discussed before we start our explanation.

1

The Modern Horse

Let us give free rein to our imagination for a moment. Just suppose we could choose and ride a horse from days gone by, for example an Olympic horse from the 1950s. What would it feel like? Inevitably, it would be a wonderful experience. We might then be tempted to ride the horse in competition with modern day horses to see how it compared. What a challenge! Unfortunately, we would then realize that in the modern competition arena we would be outclassed because although the modern horse would not score more highly on looks, elegance and suppleness, it would score more in scope and action—*power of the hindquarters*—as well as impulsion. (Note: he would also score more on the "tension" scale, too!) What happened?

Our observations are not meant as criticism. They are an attempt to find out why many horses, after a promising start in their training, develop their first motion-related problems one-and-a-half to two years later. What is the cause? The answer is that over the decades very big changes have taken place in horse breeding. Yet what has changed, in line with these developments, in the training of the horse?

TALENT CREATED BY BREEDING

The Warmblood

In Warmblood breeding, the aim of increasing and improving the horse's action seems to have been achieved. This is the result of a change in the way the hindquarters work. The modern Warmblood riding horse, and especially the competition horse, is capable of huge, powerful forward strides and movement. What does all this add up to?

The horse has been "modernized" by breeding to enable it to meet the high demands of international competition. Breeders work on the premise that success in competition is only possible if they produce exceptional horses. However, such "high powered" horses need especially skillful training. Unfortunately, in many cases, they do not seem to receive it, or at least not in our experience with the horses that have come to us with problems.

What has become apparent is that with these powerful "back-end workers," crookedness and weight on the front end *increases* rather than decreasing as training progresses. Do the

A dressage horse at the beginning of the straightness training.

The same horse after 14 days of training.

training methods in use today provide us with the means to control the centrifugal and shear forces (which will be discussed in detail later on p. 39) that result from this crookedness and being heavy in front? Should we still, with these modern horses, be placing so much emphasis on riding the horse forward?

Another question we must ask ourselves is whether we should we ride present-day horses in exactly the same way as we used to ride their counterparts 50 years ago. And, why do horses nowadays have so many movement-related and sound-ness problems, for example, knee problems?

More and more frequently these motion-related problems develop in the early stages of training—you only have to read (including between the lines) interviews in the equestrian press with otherwise successful competition riders when they talk about what has gone wrong. We cannot help but wonder what is going on when experts and trainers involved with a horse are at a loss to explain why a talented and promising horse has become irregular in its gaits for months, for example.

What seems to be happening is that people are resorting to using the many new kinds of treatment available these days as a substitute for proper training. When desperation sets in and the same old catchphrases for the various tension-related problems keep cropping up, it is time to look at the causes. When the third and fifth cervical vertebrae are being used as an excuse for a horse's problem because there is no other explana-tion, or when the real causes cannot be found or understood, we should stop and ask ourselves what is going on.

You should understand that, unlike in man, the horse's upper body—its trunk and forehand—"runs away" from its hindquarters. So, if we keep developing the pushing power of these powerful hindquarters by constantly riding the horse forward, this may encourage the horse to run away even more with its upper body from its hind end. As a result, the back muscles contract, and more and more strain is placed on them until they can no longer cope with it. It is inevitable that this will lead to serious problems, which will be discussed later (see p. 53).

The classical breeds

As with Warmbloods, the "modernization" of other breeds has advanced faster than training methods. Some experts may think it an exaggeration to say that, through breeding, these horses have been made more and more "showy," but we feel that this showiness is a major reason for the success of these breeds. Moreover, in training, the forehand tends to be the focus of attention, and the hindquarters neglected.

Compared to the Warmblood breeds, the classical breeds tend to have a higher set to the head and neck, and the muscles on the underside of the neck are more prominent. These physical characteristics, in conjunction with the action of the longissimus muscle (see drawing on p. 32 and discussion in detail on pp. 24 and 25), results in a hollowing of the horse's back. Consequently, the weight-bearing capability of the bridge (spine) between the two supports (forehand and hindquarters) is reduced.

However, since "front-heaviness" is linked to crookedness, it is reasonable to assume that in the classical breeds the problem of crookedness is even greater than in Warmbloods. Centrifugal and shear forces are therefore also more pronounced. Stress symptoms, tense steps and an "upside down" neck are a response to the action of these forces.

Much of the work produced is hurried and erratic, but onlookers and riders often fail to recognise that there is a problem because they are taken in by these horses' presence and showy way of going.

The Friesian

The behavior of the Friesian is in line with that of other classical breeds, however, we need to appreciate that this breed has very narrow bloodlines. When training them as riding horses we must never forget that these horses are bred primarily for driving, and also that there is very little scope for introducing new blood. This means great care must be taken when training them for riding, and work from the ground is invaluable. Before backing a Friesian, every effort should be made to get the crookedness under control as far as humanly possible, since high shear forces can cause knee problems, and in our experience, Friesians are prone to these. Here, as elsewhere, these problems can be avoided through proper preparation.

Shear forces are affecting this Friesian's movement (see p. 43).

2

Work to Cure

Natural

Crookedness

THE CLASSICAL TRAINING SCALE

Why should we need special training to correct the horse's crookedness when straightness is already addressed in the Six Scales of Training (as defined by the German National Equestrian Federation), and so should already form part of the horse's education?

Most dressage riders are familiar with this training ladder. It contains the steps to be followed by everyone involved in training horses, and comprises the basic elements of the horse's training. They are definitive, and we are not calling them into question. However, queries relating to the Scales of Training frequently arise, and need to be addressed. When the trainer realizes that he is not achieving the desired result with a promising horse, or when a horse suddenly and inexplicably comes to a full stop in its training, the question has to be asked: what has happened?

Now that vets are saying more and more that we do not know to what extent soundness problems are due to a horse's crookedness, it is time to take the problem seriously.

We have been asking ourselves, in the light of our experiences, whether the *order* of the Scales of Training is still correct. Modern horses have such powerful hindquarters, and so deliver such a powerful forward thrust, that *Straightness* should perhaps be first on the list.

The Training Scale

1 Rhythm

2 Suppleness

3 Contact

4 Impulsion

5 Straightness

6 Collection

Heaviness in front: it's natural!

Just as man is naturally upright, the horse is naturally "heavy in front": it carries more weight on the forehand than the hindquarters. With a young horse growing up in normal conditions with others, this causes no problems. However, for a young horse growing up alone with its mother—and sometimes only or mostly in a stall or box—being "heavy in front" may become a problem. Not only does this horse miss out on "gymnastic training" that comes from playing with other youngsters, but more especially, it does not learn about herd behavior.

Hence, both the horse's movement skills and its social behavior are affected. This often results in the horse being misunderstood, and dealing with it then requires special skills. From a physical point of view, the problem begins the moment the horse is required to carry weight; there is a risk of overtaxing it from the outset. The horse is unable to give up its "front-heavy" stance without help. It is the result of a natural instinct embedded deep within its psyche, and therefore also in its muscles. There are two logical reasons for this, the first of which is the considerable weight of its upper body, that is, of its head, neck, shoulders and rib cage. This includes the horse's organs, most of which are contained in this area.

The second reason is that the horse uses its forelegs to "feel the way" and test the ground it is treading on. Horses that do not receive sufficient preparatory training remain affected by this heaviness in front for life. The horse carries the greater proportion of its body weight on its forelegs and the rider's weight adds to this considerably. It does not take a very experienced rider to realize how much weight is then carried by the shoulders and the front feet. If you look around you can see a frightening number of horses affected by this problem.

To fully appreciate the meaning of "front-heaviness," we first need to give some thought to how the *longissimus* muscle works.

THE MEANING OF "HEAVY IN FRONT"

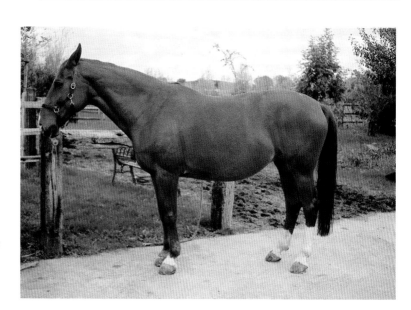

A "front-heavy" horse at the halt. The hindquarters are appreciably less developed than the shoulders. The prominent brachiocephalic (underneck) muscle and the sagging back are also clearly visible.

The *Longissimus* Muscle

The *Lehrbuch der Anatomie Haustiere* (Handbook of the Anatomy of Domestic Animals) contains the following information about the *longissimus* muscle in animals: "When acting bilaterally, it stabilizes and extends the spine, especially in the back. It actively increases the weight-bearing capacity of the back, and provides a firm basis in movement for the swinging forward or backward of the leg in the air, which is important at fast paces for hoofed animals. It acts as the elevator of the neck and head. In carnivores (animals of prey), which arch their backs very prominently at every canter stride, the powerful action of the *longissimus* muscle is clearly demonstrated as the back is straightened. Similarly, it plays an important role in the movement of horses. When weight is concentrated on the hind legs, it serves to lift the forehand when the horse rears, for example. When the weight is concentrated on the forelegs, it hollows and braces the back and lifts the hindquarters, as an example, when the horse lashes out. When acting on one side only, it bends the spine (and especially the neck) laterally, and turns the head sideways from the atlantoaxial joint." (See p. 32 for a drawing outlining the *longissimus* muscle.)

From: Nickel/Schummer/Seiferle. *Lehrbuch der Anatomie Haustiere* (Handbook of the Anatomy of Domestic Animals). 8th Edition. 2004: Parey in MVS Medizin-Verlag Stuttgart.

The Meaning of "Heavy in Front"

We are convinced that trainers do not pay enough attention to the way the horse's back works with respect to the *longissimus* muscle. So what should they be doing? Given that the *longissimus* is the only muscle to run the whole length of the horse's longitudinal axis from the atlas to the sacrum, to achieve their aim they need to work on the whole of this muscle that is, from the "steering section"—the head and neck—to the lumbar region. Because of the way the *longissimus* muscle works, the whole of the spine is involved in the transfer of weight onto the hindquarters, and then in the correction of crookedness.

How does being "heavy in front" affect the horse's training? A horse with its weight on its shoulders can lash out. More importantly, it can to stretch its head and neck upward, as when "sniffing the air." In this position, the underside of the neck stands out. It is important to realize that this is the stance connected with inner preparation for flight, and it is accompanied by the release of adrenaline, which means that the horse is going into a state of stress. So we can see that a "front-heavy" horse is almost always under stress (see drawing below).

◉ *Taking all the weight on the forelegs.*

Moreover, because of the way the *longissimus* muscle works, the back is pressed downward, so being "heavy in front" is also associated with a hollow back. This should be thoroughly understood because it explains the reasons behind a large proportion of physical problems that arise.

The back muscles become more and more contracted, resulting in restriction to the blood supply. As a result, insufficient nutrients are available. Slowly but surely, metabolism breaks down. Hence the hollowed back is accompanied by muscle wastage. The strain on joints, including those of the spine, is enormous, and can lead to the condition known as "kissing spines." The abdominal muscles sag as well as the back muscles, and the middle of the horse's body takes on the appearance of a suspension bridge.

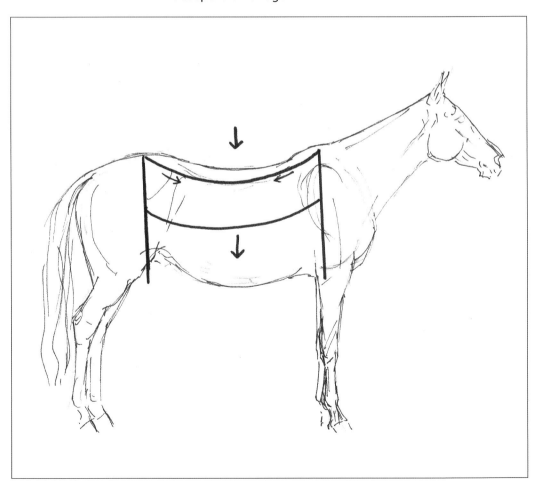

Q & A

Question:
Why does the horse not do something about its hollow back since it is uncomfortable or even hurts?

Answer:
The horse stays like this because it is "programmed" into him, that is, it is instinctive. This incorrect way of going is so ingrained into its mind that there is a psychological aspect to the problem. So unless he's been "made" to change, he stays like this.

The loins—the weak link

Another problem area in all mammals is the loins. In man, the area comprising the five lumbar vertebrae is a well-known source of serious problems, and many people have a story to tell about this part of their body! It is the weak point in the spine, because there are only these five vertebrae, supported by muscles, ligaments and tendons to connect the upper body to the lower body. The balancing pole of the upper body attaches to and moves from the pelvis, guided by the brain and the sense of balance (see adjoining drawing).

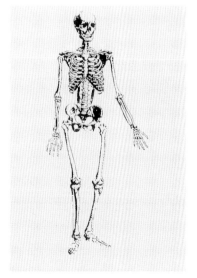

As an experiment, take a look at a human being on all fours in a horizontal position. This is more or less the equivalent of the horse's stance. In this position, you become very aware of your loins, and how weak they are, yet every movement of the shoulders depends on the unconscious support of the lumbar area.

Since horses and other four-legged animals, unlike man, are permanently in a horizontal position, the forelegs serve to support the upper body. In other words, the

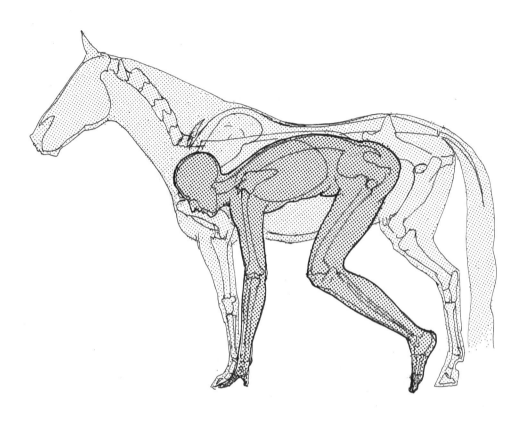

The loins: the weak point in both horse and man.

forelegs play their part in allowing the horse to keep its balance. It might also be said that since the horse uses its forelegs to help support itself, the part of the brain that is responsible for balance is not so highly developed as in man.

In the horse, as in man, movement of the shoulders triggers a reaction in the loins. This is of fundamental importance. You should give serious thought to this, and make a comparison with your own body. Placing weight on the horse in the shoulder region requires a tightening of the muscles in its loins. For example, when the horse is very heavy in front, the work of the lumbar muscles increases considerably. Moreover, if the *longissimus* muscle is weak, the horse's back sags in the area that comprises the six lumbar vertebrae.

The Meaning of "Heavy in Front"

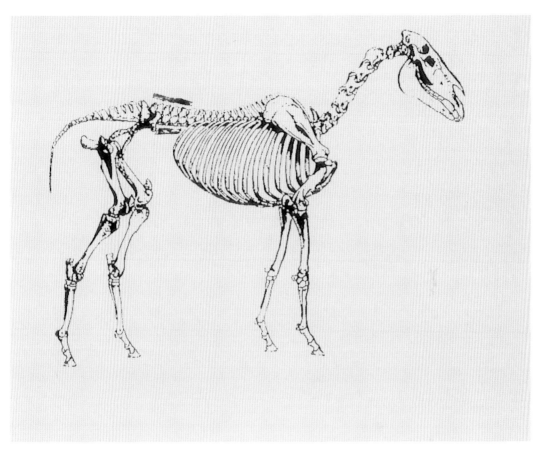

◑ The lumbar spine is marked
above and below by thick lines.

Note

On the subject of "kissing spines," the condition mentioned on p. 26: horse owners are often wrongly advised that horses suffering from this condition should be ridden forward and downward, possibly through the use of draw reins and auxiliary aids. But you will never get anywhere with training while the back is "swinging downward" because of the horse being "front-heavy."

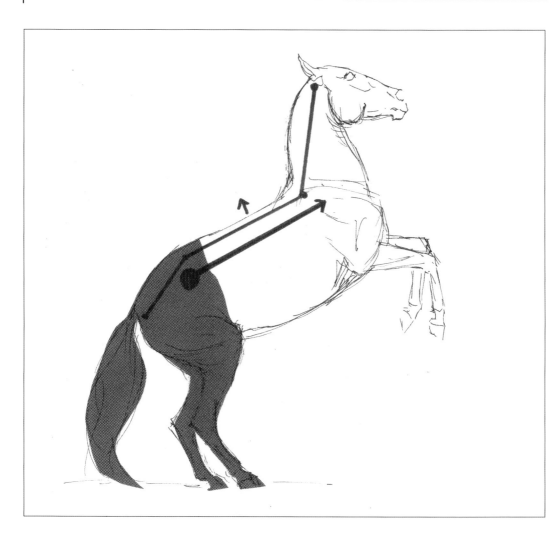

● *Taking all the weight on the hind legs.*

When a horse rears, it takes all the weight on the hind legs. However, in training you must always strive to get the horse to take more of its weight on its hindquarters to enable it to carry you properly and to "work from behind." In days gone by, the activity of the hindquarters was developed through work between two wooden pillars: the horse was attached on both sides to a pillar, and then driven forward. The aim was to make the horse's back swing upward—the only way to take the strain off its joints and give the rider the feeling of being carried. To this day, this is still the aim of training, and is particularly important with modern horses. Unfortunately, however, it is seldom achieved.

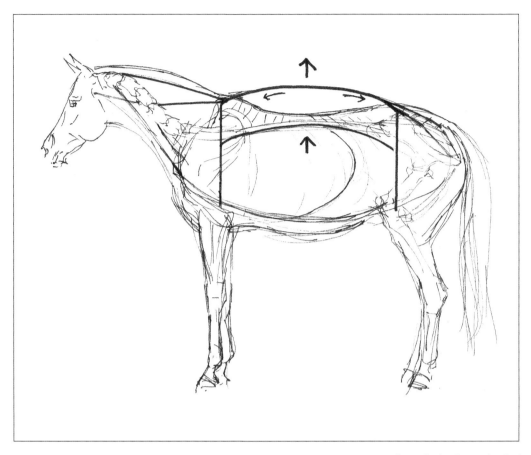

 The arched or hump-backed bridge effect.

Note

The whole of the flexible section of the back between the front and hind legs, which we can call the "bridging pillars," must swing upward like an arched or hump-backed bridge (see drawing above). The difficult area, from a training point of view, is the part where the flexible section of the spine joins the relatively inflexible withers. It takes time for the longissimus muscle to "de-contract" (and so lengthen) at this point owing to the rigidity of this part of the body, and stiffening and resistance are often encountered.

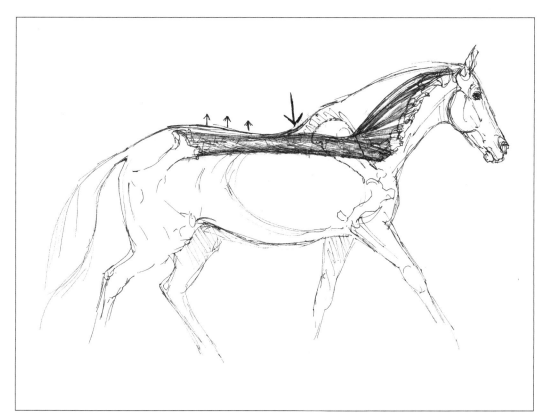

Working through the back: getting the horse to soften and "let go" at the point just behind the withers is the slowest and most difficult part of training. The longissimus muscle is shown in the shaded color.

In almost all the clinics we hold at home and abroad, the first day is taken up with diagnosing the problems of the horses that have been brought to us. As we do at home, we record each new horse on video and use the video footage to explain the horse's way of going to the riders. This is a good introduction to the clinic, and is accompanied by a talk on the subject of crookedness and how to deal with it. We include discussion on how the longissimus muscle works, and the problems that arise in connection with it. Unfortunately, we are seldom, if ever, brought a horse with an upward swinging back, so when we are asked, "Show us what you mean by the back 'swinging upward': what should it look like?" we have to demonstrate using video footage of horses that have been successfully "treated" using our system. The initial reaction is usually utter amazement: what we are trying to explain is unheard of! It comes as quite a shock. What is this upward-swinging back? Riders are frequently unfamiliar with the way a horse can move when its back is swinging upward as it should.

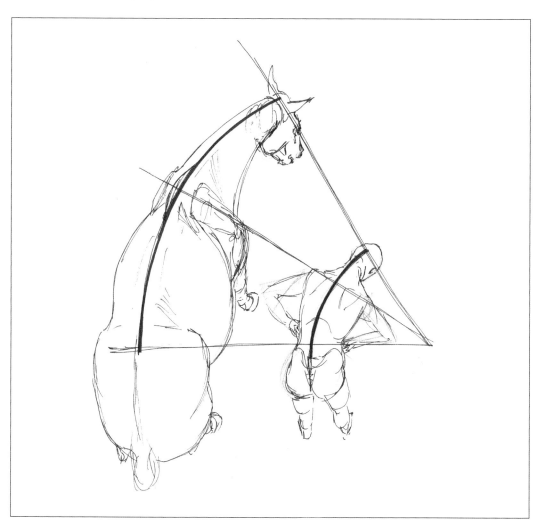

Ideal bend.

This drawing demonstrates the lateral bend function of the *longissimus* muscle. It is with this (proceeding with great care) that we can do the most to reduce heaviness on the forehand and inborn crookedness. We use the word "reduce" on purpose, since crookedness is a natural characteristic, and cannot be eliminated completely.

INBORN CROOKEDNESS

Naturally occurring

Crookedness is the second of the distinctive, inborn characteristics that affect the horse's motion. In our experience, it affects motion to an even greater extent than heaviness on the forehand. We consider crookedness even more dangerous since riders and trainers often do not realize the effects that it has on the horse's body if it is not corrected.

First of all, let's clarify what is meant by natural crookedness. How do we define it? Does it occur only in horses? The answer to the latter is a definite "no." It affects *all* mammals, including man. It has received a lot of publicity in various equine publications recently, and has been the subject of many very different and complicated explanations. In fact, it is simply "right-" or "left-handedness," that is, forelimb dominance. Just as man has more confidence in his right or left hand in critical situations, the horse "puts its best foot forward," using its best foreleg to get itself out of trouble. This entails putting more weight onto the shoulder on the same side (see the drawings on pp. 35 and 37). The result is the horse becomes crooked.

To make the problem easier to understand, in this book we will refer to crookedness as natural. Our observations on the subject are based on extensive experience gained at our Center predominantly with horses brought to us because the owners had "tried everything," or because training had reached a "dead end." Often, veterinary treatment had been tried—and had failed—because no one realized that crookedness was the cause of the horse's problems.

As we've explained, this natural crookedness is indeed a *big* problem. Let us start by assuming that 70 percent of all people are right-handed, and 30 percent are left-handed. In horses, the percentage is almost identical. You must also understand that in man, the degree of right- or left-handedness varies with the individual, that is, it is more or less pronounced. The same applies to the horse, though man's influence over this natural crookedness may increase, or may develop into *acquired* crookedness.

In the explanation that follows, we base all our explanations on the larger group, the right-handed or right-forelimb-dominant horses. Obviously, all applies equally to the other 30 to 40 percent, the left-handed group. We rarely find horses that are naturally straight.

So, to say it again, natural crookedness is more or less pronounced depending on the individual. It is present in every young horse from the outset. How this crookedness affects each horse individually must be understood if you are to be able to tackle the problems caused by it. When a rider's weight is added to the equation, the imbalance of weight on one side is increased drastically. We believe that if this natural crookedness is not recognized and greatly reduced, it can lead to the development of navicular disease in later life. Our experience shows this to be the case. Direct and intensive collaboration involving the veterinary practitioner, a skilled farrier and a competent trainer is required.

Natural crookedness results in various stresses and forms of tension that affect different horses in very different ways. It is also logical that as a result of this crookedness there will be powerful lateral forces acting on the spine. It is obvious that the solution lies in getting rid of the cause rather than treating the resulting problems.

For example, rhythm faults originating in the right shoulder and foreleg are probably the result of natural crookedness, which leads us to another serious problem that arises: if the horse is "leaning," that is, placing excessive weight on its right shoulder, it will take a slightly shorter step with its right foreleg (see drawing on p. 36). Consequently—and this is very important—the right hind leg will also shorten its step. The horse drags the right hind leg, at first almost imperceptibly, but then more and more. This is because when the horse is leaning on its right shoulder, there is less impetus for the right hindquarter and hind leg to move, and consequently the hind leg drags behind. We have seen cases—and these are not uncommon—where horses have been given chiropractic manipulation treatment on their knee ligaments to try to cure this problem. (You can make your own judgment about this!) In such cases, as with people, a lasting solution can only be achieved through appropriate gymnastic training. In short, "leaning" on one or other of the shoulders causes a constant strain, which

A crooked horse "putting its best foot forward" and placing extra weight on it: in a right-handed horse, the weight falls forward diagonally from the left hind foot to the right forefoot. The only way to correct this is to shift the excess weight back across this diagonal so the inside hind leg can step forward underneath and lighten the right shoulder. For the complete sequence showing this, see pp. 62–3.

must eventually harm the horse. The rider's weight inevitably makes the problem worse, especially if he is inexperienced and has not yet learned to control where to place it. A supposedly experienced rider may mistakenly try to "hold up" the shoulder that the horse is leaning on. This simply makes the problem worse in the long run. It is difficult for a crooked horse to carry its rider. As a result, it becomes nervous, and this seriously affects its training: a horse whose natural crookedness is not corrected becomes mentally unstable. Its mind will not accept training. Its long-term performance capability is reduced in proportion to the crookedness that remains. This, in itself, ought to be good enough reason not to hurry training. Of course, it is possible to make a horse "rideable" in a very short period of time, but only if it is understood that within two years at most, its natural crookedness will start to take its toll. And of course, in the meantime, the horse will have problems turning to one side and not move well on that rein. It has its "bad side."

Before discussing this subject in detail, we must understand and agree on some basic principles. In the chapters that follow, we will be talking about crookedness and the problems that arise from it. We'll also keep referring to the subject of right- and left-handedness, though to avoid confusion, remember that all discussion will be about a right-handed meaning a right-forelimb-dominant horse.

The "right-handed" horse "leans" on its right shoulder automatically and takes a shorter step with its right foreleg. This, in its turn, causes the right hind leg to shorten its step. You can understand this if you walk leaning on a stick held in your right hand: you will see straightaway that your right leg is taking shorter steps.

First, certain questions that must be answered:

What is the connection between "heavy in front" and crookedness?

Heaviness on the forehand and crookedness are directly related. There is no crookedness without heaviness in front.

What is natural inborn crookedness?

Let us start from the assumption that in a straight horse the center of balance (or, center of gravity) lies at the intersection of the two diagonal lines shown in the drawing below.

   Crookedness is characterized by the center of balance being displaced forward and to the right (in a right-handed horse). In other words, it is displaced forward along a diagonal line drawn from the left hindquarter to the right shoulder (see drawing below).

SOME BASIC QUESTIONS

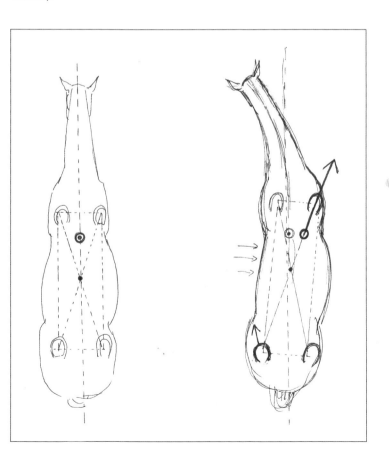

Crookedness involves loss of balance across the diagonal, i.e. in a right-handed horse onto the right shoulder. The big arrow represents this movement of the weight onto the right shoulder. The horse's normal reaction is to carry the head and neck to the opposite side to counteract this excess weight on the right shoulder. This causes it to be concave on its left side (shown by the small arrows).

How do you introduce a young horse to corrective longe work?

Opinions differ widely on this subject. Our own viewpoint is that a young horse with its inherent problems such as crookedness and heaviness on the forehand is actually easier to straighten, and more easily made to change its weight distribution, than an older animal. This is because the mind of a young horse has not been influenced by previous training. Moreover, the horse is free from tension and problems that the weight of the rider causes. An appropriate age to begin this longe training is between two and three years. This early "gymnastic" training must not be confused with backing and riding the horse, which are obviously things we would not do so young. The work we do on the longe is aimed simply at *straightening* the horse and getting it to take more of its weight onto its hindquarters.

The young horse is then put back into a group of horses to allow it to play and it is then that the benefits of the early gymnastic training quickly become apparent. Its increased athleticism and agility, and improved use of its hindquarters allow it to improve its position in the herd. It becomes more self-confident, and it is mentally well-adjusted.

How can a rider recognize the signs of his horse's crookedness?

The easiest way to identify crookedness is on the circle when the horse comes away from the wall: on the left rein (with a right-handed horse) the circle gets bigger, and on the right rein the horse falls into the circle. As a general rule this applies to any turns, bends and curved tracks.

What forces arise as a result of crookedness, and how do they affect the horse's training?

We must pause at this point, because in our experience, the forces that arise as a result of crookedness is one of the most important issues, and one that gives rise to many a misunderstanding and wrong assessment during the horse's training. You need to understand, first of all, that all mammals have a tendency to overbalance in a forward direction, or "fall forward," which triggers a powerful reaction in the hindquarters.

If you are to tackle the causes of the problem rather than just treat the symptoms, you need to understand this reaction. To do this, you need to examine the two basic forces to which the horse's natural crookedness give rise, namely *centrifugal* force and *shear* force (see diagrams on pp. 41–2 and 44).

Note

Every horse has to contend with centrifugal and shear forces.

CENTRIFUGAL AND SHEAR FORCES

A right-handed horse going on the left rein. In this photo, the lines indicate the position of its center of gravity.

The dotted line clearly shows how this horse is "falling out through its right shoulder," as a result of centrifugal force.

The size of the circle is irrelevant here. The centrifugal force is triggered by the right outside shoulder falling out, which makes the horse concave to the left.

When the outside shoulder falls out, the rest of the body must follow. A speed skater has the same problem when he comes to a bend on the track. So to counteract the centrifugal force and avoid being pulled outward off the track, he crosses one leg in front of the other. The horse behaves in a similar way, as shown by the way it puts down its front and hind feet.

This picture of the same right-handed horse on a left rein shows how centrifugal force acts on the hindquarters. The arrows indicate how the right hind leg is about to go "wide" toward the outside edge of the ring.

There is another phenomenon that occurs, and it has to do with the pull on the longissimus muscle. This is important because it affects the area that is most commonly targeted for treatment—the third and fifth neck vertebrae. Pain in this area is often attributed to the horse having had a fall at some time or having got itself caught up in something. Of course, it's possible the horse had an accident, but in view of the frequency of the problem, this diagnosis should be treated with suspicion.

Let us try to illustrate this. When the right-handed horse is turning to the left, and centrifugal force is causing it to fall out through its right shoulder, the *longissimus* muscle is stretched on the right side. The pull increases to the point where the horse is, as it were, "hanging on" to the now over-tense muscle. This places enormous strain on the spine laterally, from left to right.

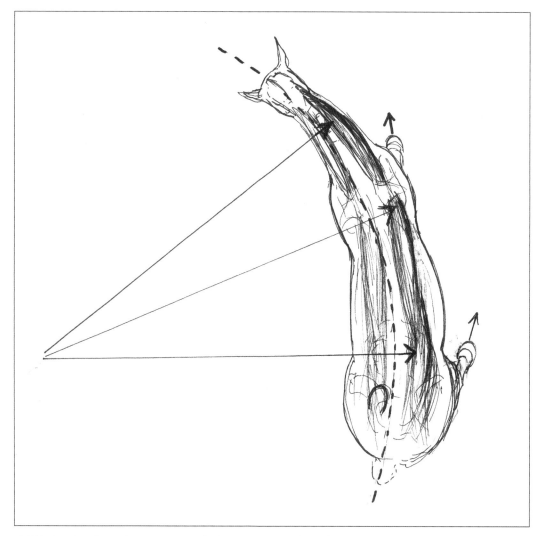

⬭ *This drawing shows the strain put on the longissimus muscle on the right side.*

Overstretching leads to tension, which cannot help but affect the skeleton, or in this case the spine (see drawing below). As is to be expected, the parts of the spine most affected are those that are unsupported, the cervical and lumbar vertebrae. These have no defence against the effects of the overstretched *longissimus* muscle. This is the cause of the so-called "third and fifth neck vertebrae syndrome."

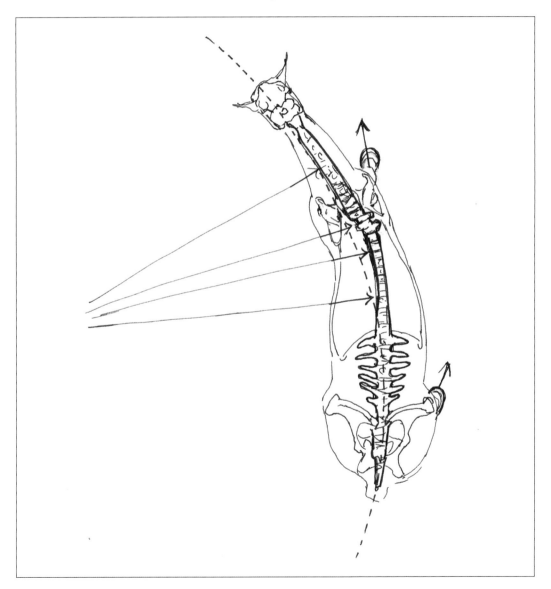

The action of centrifugal force on the skeleton of a right-handed horse.

Apart from the strain on the right forefoot (as shown in the photos on p. 39 and the drawing on p. 41), which bears most of the brunt of centrifugal forces, there is constant strain on the tendons, navicular bone, and spine. Damage is caused that costs many horses their lives. This is why it is important for everyone who is involved with horses to be aware of some of the consequences of crookedness. (For more on this, see *Tina Rasch, Veterinary Practitioner,* p. 117.)

Shear forces

Negative though the effects are from *centrifugal* forces, when *shear* forces come into play, the situation can be worse. Unlike centrifugal force, the horse cannot control shear forces. It is at the mercy of them, and it needs to be helped. Working on the right rein (with a right-handed horse) is where the action of the shear forces is particularly pronounced.

In the photos below, the horse is "leaning" on its right front foot and, in order to keep its balance is twisting the rest of its body–its hindquarters–round its right foreleg.

〠 *A right-handed horse on the right rein, showing the effects of shear forces on its hindquarters. The shaded area is the distance that the hind leg is thrown outward.*

〠 *A right-handed horse on the right rein: the horse is placing excess weight on its right forefoot. The vertical and horizontal lines represent the horse's ideal position. The oblique line runs through the shoulder joints and shows their deviation from the horizontal, so the shaded area is the angle at which the horse is leaning to the right.*

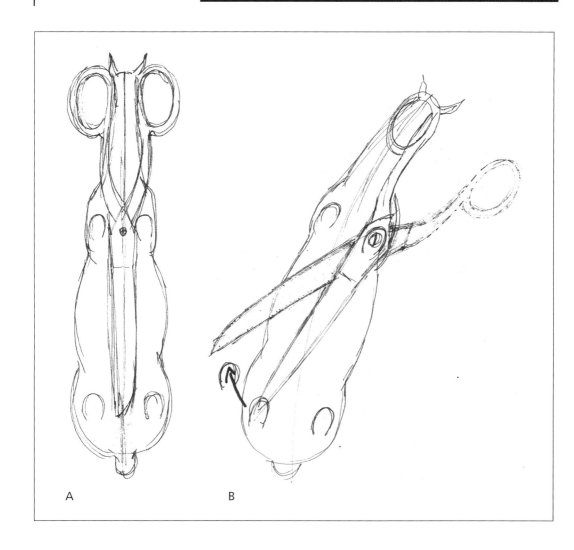

A   B

Shear force is illustrated here by the action of a pair of scissors. Drawing (B) shows how the center of gravity shifts onto the right shoulder when the horse moves, causing the hindquarters to "shear away" to the outside.

To explain shear force in the horse: similar to a pair of scissors, one of the blades (sides of the horse) remains fixed while the other "shears away" diagonally (see drawing above). Since the horse's joints are designed for carrying it *forward* rather than making this sort of movement, the consequences are serious.

Shear forces place enormous strain on the contact surfaces of the joints and on the ligaments associated with these joints. The most commonly encountered consequences are knee and hock problems and changes in the inside hind leg resulting in short or even spasmodic steps.

Centrifugal and Shear Forces

Shear forces also place considerable strain on the sacroiliac joint. And, we could go on adding to this list indefinitely! All these symptoms result in loss of balance and cause irreparable harm.

Let us take the stifle, for example. As the body turns around the right foreleg, which is on the ground for longest time, the hindquarters "shear away" to the left. (Horses that move in this way are also weak in their hindquarters.) The weight of the back part of the horse's body then falls on the first joint of the left hind leg, that is, the stifle. This stretches or places enormous strain on tendons and ligaments, and may loosen the patella (see photos on p. 43).

Another symptom is taking shorter steps with one hind leg. In the right-handed horse, it is nearly always the right hind leg that takes the shorter step. This is because the arc traveled by the right shoulder is foreshortened, as shown in the drawing below.

The foreshortened arc traveled by the right shoulder in a right-handed horse.

A right-handed horse puts the right forefoot down more quickly, so the right shoulder has to come down at a steeper angle. The horse places its weight onto the right shoulder, the right hind leg cannot reach far enough forward, and the result is the step is shortened. This is another problem that is misinterpreted, and so dealt with incorrectly. For example, it is often diagnosed as a crooked pelvis, but this condition simply does not exist on the scale we see this happening!

Of course, a crooked pelvis can occur, but 95 percent of the problems diagnosed as such are simply due to one shoulder being lower than the other. The recommended way to deal with this is through appropriate training—*straightness training!*

Straightness training

As we've made clear, in this book we are focusing on the concepts of heaviness on the forehand and natural crookedness in the horse. It is the problems that arise from these conditions that have led us to develop a corrective method: our system of straightness training.

To begin, we longe the horse, but the work we do with the horse on the longe is different from what is commonly understood as "longe work." Instead, we give the horse "corrective treatment" or "corrective training." What are we doing? We are setting out to change the horse's way of going, and we do this by influencing the position of its center of gravity. *This is what is required to make the horse straight.*

As mentioned, the horse is by nature a creature of flight. In the wild or when turned out in the field, it moves at different speeds for different purposes related to its survival. To make our work easier to understand, let us examine the opposite extremes of the horse's movement. At one end of the spectrum is flight, which is the response to the ultimate stress-situation. The horse is in a state of panic, fearing for its life.

At the other end is the horse's personal, "economy" speed. This is adopted when the horse is under no pressure, for example, when trotting to a different position in the field or making its way to the waterhole or trough in the morning or evening. This has the lowest requirement in terms of energy, and the horse is relaxed and moves freely through its back. Hence, moving through the back is a natural characteristic.

However, when in training, the horse is required to work at a set tempo, which lies between these two *natural* "speeds." This means that during the training phase, the trainer must help the horse understand what is required and avoid triggering the "flight" response.

Corrective training consists, first of all, in taking the horse back to its leisurely, "economy" speed. We call it the horse's "personal" speed because it varies greatly from one horse to the next, and is also influenced by breeding.

This is the simplest way to influence the position of its center of gravity. Once the horse is in balance, its stress level falls, and shear force and centrifugal force no longer come into play. It is then that the horse really "lets go" and begins to swing through its back. At this point, and only then, can the horse develop its performance skills and begin to fulfill its potential.

All young, unbroken horses should be trained in this way as a matter of course to enable them to become light and responsive to the aids. Many of the horses we have worked with and managed to cure were in a permanent stressed state when they came to us, because their riders lacked the necessary "feel," and had never managed to ride them forward and downward in the correct way. Using the horse's personal "economy speed" to teach it to go forward and downward is the only way to get out of trouble.

At the Center, we usually allocate about four weeks for this corrective training. This is on the basis that the horse will then be on the right track, and the rider will be able to continue the training alone. Obviously, this is just the start: in four weeks, change can only be "introduced."

We'd like to bring your attention again to the developments that have taken place over the last 50 years in breeding. It must be understood that the powerful hindquarters of the modern horse must be taken into account if problems are to be avoided. In our opinion, breeding should be geared to training, and vice versa.

What are we trying to achieve with our corrective training? It can be summarized fairly simply as follows: we want the horse's

> **Note**
>
> For a "horizontal" animal such as the horse, the position of its center of gravity is less of an issue than it is for the "vertical" animal such as man. This is because it uses its "hands" to help balance itself.

hind feet to follow in the same tracks as the forefeet, and its back to swing upward. This is our aim, because only then will the horse be able to work forward and downward without the use of artificial aids.

It is up to man (the vertical animal) to help the horse (the horizontal animal). This help consists in teaching the horse, in its horizontal position, to perform movements that are "anatomically correct." In our opinion, it is easier to do this without weight on the horse's back. This is why the horse should be worked from the ground on the longe *before* it is ridden.

What problems can this create? As you know, horses are designed to flee in a straight line—not to run round in circles! So, what does this mean for the rider? It means that you have to get the horse to carry itself with its hindquarters instead of propping itself up with its forehand. It also means that its weight on the forehand must be moved *diagonally* backward so that it is carried by the hindquarters. Only by bending the horse, that is, on circles and curved tracks, can the horse's weight be transferred onto the hindquarters (see pp. 62–3). The horse can *only* become straight when it has learned *on the circle* to use its inside hind leg to support its inside shoulder (and inside hindquarter). We are certain that classical school figures and exercises still in use today are based on the realization that bending the horse makes it possible to influence the shoulders and to activate the hindquarters.

What are other aims of our corrective training? We must not forget the influence of crookedness on the horse's metabolism. As we keep mentioning, crookedness leads to tension. This tension affects the whole body. The blood supply to the muscles is restricted more and more, which affects the metabolic process accordingly. This in turn causes a further deterioration in the horse's performance. The horse sweats more readily and gives off a sour smell. It no longer has that pleasant odor typical of the healthy horse.

Very crooked horses do not breath deeply enough. We can all understand this from our own experience: when we are very tense, we become short of breath. It is the same with the horse. The muscles then receive insufficient oxygen, which results in stress and circulatory problems, the horse's performance suffers, and it will only go forward when driven.

Our training involves both preventing and curing these problems. And, whilst on this subject we must also mention that tension problems originating in pain (for example, after an operation or the birth of a foal*) can be cured quite quickly with our methods. The horse is then able to return to its previous level of performance. Appropriate gymnastic exercises have been shown to give excellent results in such cases. It is often better to begin the exercises at an early stage rather than leave the horse in the field for months. The horse is an athlete, and recovers faster through exercise.

*Mares should not be ridden after foaling until their back has been strengthened through exercises.

3

The Diagnosis

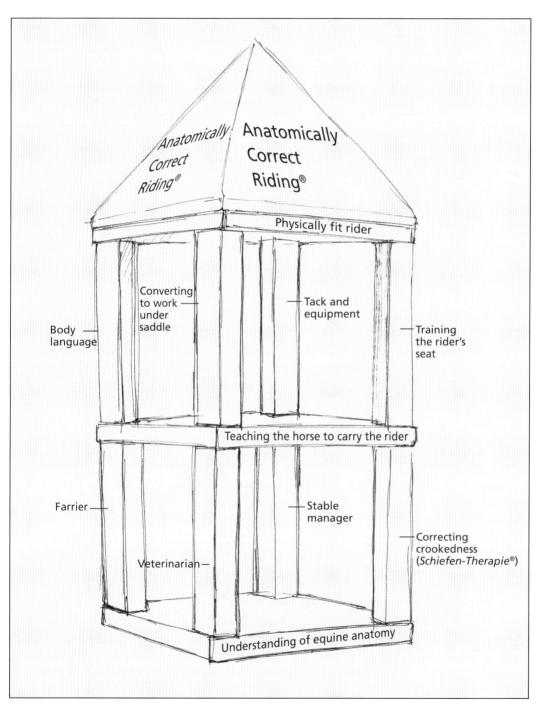

Anatomically Correct Riding (ARR®) is the framework. All professionals necessary for the horse's training are brought together under one roof.

AN INTEGRATED HOLISTIC APPROACH

This diagram (p. 51) illustrates our *integrated,* or to describe it another way, our "holistic" (meaning "whole") approach, and shows how everything fits together. Only when all the "pillars" are in position is the "building" firm and stable.

Knowledge of equine anatomy is the foundation of the building. Every horseman should have a basic understanding of the physical criteria the horse needs to meet in order to carry the rider without harm to itself. This is the basis of training.

The "ground floor"

At our Center, the farrier who examines and, if necessary, corrects the horse's foot, is just as important as the veterinary specialist. These two "pillars" need to be in place before a diagnosis can be made. The veterinary aspect is important because no horse is allowed to begin its straightness training without being given the "all clear" to proceed.

Then the *first stage* (and most important part) of the corrective training begins, which is the corrective work on the longe. This is carried out by our professional trainers, and takes from two to three weeks, depending on problems encountered. The horse must be given sufficient training to ensure that there is no danger of it reverting to its previous behavior. The idea is that when the rider takes over again, the problems have already been solved.

This brings us to an important point. The rider must be prepared to learn *from* the horse that has now been changed in its way of going before he can take over. It is not easy to make a rider understand this.

This first stage is complete when the horse is standing in front of us, able and ready to carry the rider. (For a thorough explanation of this stage, see chapter 4, *Correcting Crookedness: Practical Work*.) Reaching this stage is an achievement in itself, but it is also essential as a foundation for further training, or just as correct basic training. Everybody involved at our Center is well aware that this fresh start can only be achieved through a joint effort. The next step is to "translate" the work on the ground into work under saddle.

The "top floor"

It is the rider who plays the main part in the *second stage* of the corrective training. For this stage to commence, certain pre-conditions must be met. At the Center, before the rider sits on the newly straightened horse, the tack is scrutinized by an expert. Attention is paid to all equipment, but especially the saddle. It is quite incredible how often people change their saddle, frequently with the fitting entrusted to so-called "experts" who may not have the necessary experience. We always enlist the help of a highly qualified saddler to perform this assessment.

Another pre-condition is "retraining" the rider's seat. Sometimes, the rider needs to learn what he thinks he already knows because once the horse's corrective training is complete he will find he now has a horse that works as it should—through its back, with rhythm and impulsion. It helps when the rider "knows" his own body. As a result of what he observed during the *first stage*—the corrective straightness training from the ground—together with this new seat training, he gains an awareness of the horse's balance. He can begin to develop a new feel for the horse and its movement. This transition from work on the ground to work under saddle is important. Its sole purpose is to teach the rider how to ride his right-handed (or left-handed) horse on the right rein, and how to ride it on the left rein. However, the ultimate aim is to incorporate this work into the horse's general training. This should make it easier for the rider to tie in what he has learned at the Center with the work that he does with the horse at home.

Usually, when people come to us they have tried nearly everything to help their horse but found it impossible to discover, or sort out the problem. Veterinary medicine, osteopathy, physiotherapy, and other therapists have not produced the desired results—all have run out of ideas. It is at this point that we become involved, and suggest to the rider that the problems must be crookedness. So that the rider can properly understand corrective training, first, we like to demonstrate the problem.

The first part of the diagnosis is made with the horse standing still. We ask the rider to bring the results of any previous

THE

PHYSICAL

EXAM

tests, such as X-rays. There are always members of our veterinary team present, since, as we mentioned earlier, the horse can only proceed to the corrective training phase when it receives the "green light."

The horse is examined literally from head to toe. This gives us all the necessary information about its body: we detect any tension, check the stability of the knee region, look at the way the horse carries its head and neck, examine its back, compare the forehand and hindquarters, and check the shoeing. At the

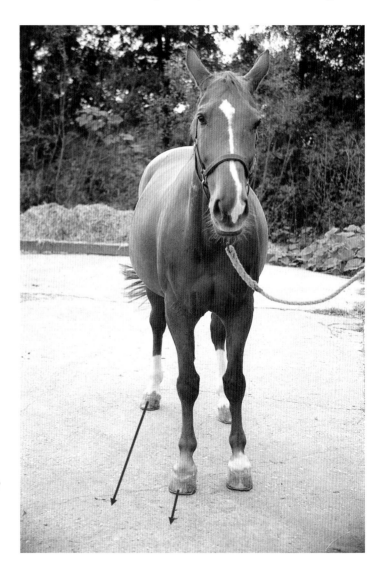

A right-handed horse. The effects of centrifugal forces are evident even when the horse is standing still: both its right front foot and right hind foot angle to the right.

same time, we try to establish whether the horse is left- or right-handed.

All our observations are then checked again with the horse in motion, because the information we have gained so far may be misleading due to tension in the muscles, for example. We discuss the assessment with the rider as we go along. For this diagnosis, the horse is fitted with a cavesson and longe line.

The next step is to film the horse moving with a digital video camera. This is very important for the rider. We do this in our longeing arena. The problems show up better there, because the effects of centrifugal and shear forces are easier to see when the horse is on a small circle—10 or 11 meters in diameter. We begin this diagnosis of the horse in motion on a circle in the direction of the non-dominant forelimb, that is, to the left with a right-handed horse.

A question we are often asked is why we start off by longeing the horse with a much more pronounced lateral bend (on the small circle) than will be required of it in later training. We need to do this for videoing purposes because the horse's reaction to the request to travel on such a small circle shows its problems really well. Since we only do this for a short time, it will not harm the horse. By making this extreme demand, we are "asking the horse a question." The "answer" is usually clear for all to see: the horse tells us what it cannot do on each rein. Its negative reactions, triggered by centrifugal and shear forces, are the subject of the first part of the discussion—involving all concerned—that takes place immediately afterward while watching the video. Through the use of slow motion and freeze frame technology, a detailed analysis of the horse's movement is carried out. The way the horse picks up and sets down each foot clearly demonstrates the stress being placed on it during work.

The direction of movement of the horse's back can also be seen on the video, and the forces exerted on the joints by its "downward-swinging back" putting weight onto the forehand (see p. 77 for discussion of why this is so detrimental) are visible. Of course, the action of these forces on the spine is particularly pronounced. Further strain is placed on the spine through the contraction of the *longissimus* muscle, as was discussed in the last chapter (p. 25). The connective tissue between the vertebral bodies, which should serve as a buffer against downward pressure by expanding and contracting like a sponge with the up and down movement, can no longer do its job properly. This results in pain and can lead, as mentioned before, to the condition known as "kissing spines." At some point in this discussion, it is often argued that there is no such thing as a "downward-swinging back," that is, if the back is moving in a downward direction it cannot be described as "swinging." However, about 80 percent of riders believe their horse is swinging *through* its back, when in fact the back is swinging *downward*. They do not understand the difference between an upward- and a downward-swinging back. This sometimes makes our discussion difficult!

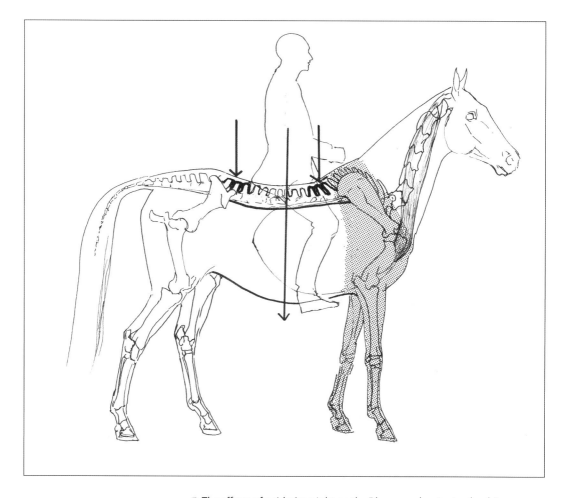

The effects of a rider's weight on the "downward-swinging back."

If the back and abdominal muscles are weak, the rider becomes a burden.

So, our "question" to the horse has received an "answer," which the rider has usually already suspected, but this is the first time he has been able to see it quite so clearly. Most riders are now also fully aware that the horse makes these incorrect movements consistently, every time it is worked. Centrifugal and shear forces come into play whenever it turns or makes a circle. *This is what happens when straightness has not been taught as it should have been—at the start of training!*

Having said all this, however, why is it that even the dressage horses competing at international level have difficulty keeping their hindquarters in line with their forehand on curves, turns and circles, and going accurately through corners? We should give this matter some thought and be prepared to look further into it. To put it another way, when these videos reveal the real causes of the horse's problems, we again see the proof of what

BALANCE, CENTER OF GRAVITY AND CROOKEDNESS

we have been saying all along: namely that *90 to 95 percent of motion-related problems are due to the horse's natural crookedness,* that the consequences of centrifugal and shear forces cause enormous strain on the joints, and when muscles get tired, on the bones, too.

The rider now has a logical explanation of the problems in his horse's way of going. The next step is to discuss what needs to be done to improve the horse's movement, and to put this training plan into practice.

After the initial diagnosis of inborn crookedness, people tend to react by asking, "How can I get rid of the problem?" However, without an answer to the question "Why does it happen?" there can be no satisfactory answer to "How?"

We consider that balance and crookedness are interconnected. They may even be one and the same. One thing, though, is certain: balance has a direct influence on the horse's mind. A horse that is not in balance is unsure of itself and becomes nervous.

The unbalanced horse is not fully in control of its body. The problem increases with the addition of the rider's weight. The horse is constantly "chasing" its shifting center of gravity. Where does the center of gravity keep going? The answer is to be found in the natural behavior of a four-legged animal, that is, a creature such as the horse that uses its forelegs for support.

In critical situations, the horse always reacts in the same way. It adopts the position in which it feels most secure. With a right-handed horse, this entails placing its weight over the right forefoot. We react in the same way when we lose our balance. For example, when we trip, we steady ourself with our right hand if we are right-handed. This is known as a "reaction" because in moments such as this we do not have time to think what we are doing; we respond automatically. Like the horse, we become nervous because we have lost control of our body.

What for us is only an occasional occurrence is an ongoing situation for a horse that has never been trained to be straight. How many riders, even experienced ones, misinterpret their horse's nervousness? How often do we hear people say "He's not concentrating, make him listen," and "He's not with it today, wake him up," or "He's messing with you, show him who's boss."

Balance, Center of Gravity and Crookedness

We need to ask ourselves whether the horse is really not listening, or so hard-mouthed, or whether perhaps its behavior is caused by it being constantly out of balance. We need to think carefully about the meaning of balance. If we do not understand crookedness and the influence of the center of gravity, our responses to his behavior will probably be incorrect.

Balance = equilibrium = a correctly positioned,
stable center of gravity

Once we start to take the subject of balance seriously, we begin to be able to deal with many of the problems that we thought were beyond our control. There are any number of gadgets and accessories available to help with handling, or specifically aimed at solving control problems, but these are no substitute for studying the subject of balance. Getting to grips with balance problems makes the rider steadier, which, in turn, helps with the task ahead. Balance makes everything easier, more relaxed, and more enjoyable for horse and rider, which is how it should be.

We cannot discuss balance and center of gravity without mentioning the role of the shoulders. Is there a direct connection between the shoulders and center of gravity? If so, when the horse loses its balance in a forward direction by "falling onto its forehand," it means that its center of gravity also moves forward toward the shoulders.

It follows from this that if the center of gravity is on or near the shoulders, it must be possible to influence and control it through the shoulders. So, is riding the horse *forward* the answer to crookedness problems? Surely then, we should be paying much more attention during training to the shoulders and forehand, especially when dealing with the modern horse which, as we have mentioned before, delivers such a powerful thrust with its hindquarters. However, this can only work if you also develop the activity of the hindquarters through a special program of training, which we like to call "interval training."

A horse that's not in balance cannot move freely and "through" its back.

Or, saying the same thing a different way:

A crooked horse cannot move freely and "through" its back.

On the ground, work *from the front backward*, so that under saddle you can work *forward from behind*.

With most of the horses that come to the Center, we find that in their previous training not enough attention has been paid to the shoulders. We could go so far as to say that the shoulders have been ignored completely. Yet it is what the horse is doing with its shoulders that causes the dreaded centrifugal and shear forces. The behavior of the shoulders also has serious consequences for the hindquarters, and all future training therefore becomes difficult. A horse that has not been taught to be straight lacks rhythm and impulsion, does not work through its back, cannot develop a correct contact, and certainly cannot work with the desired ease and lightness.

DIAGONAL IMBALANCE

Diagonal balance is a concept that everyone seems to understand in itself, but if we bring crookedness into the equation, things become more complicated. We cannot repeat often enough that *man, as a "vertical" animal finds it difficult to think, or indeed feel, "horizontally"*!

Where can we see an example of diagonal loss of balance? It is most obvious in trot since the feet are picked up and set down in diagonal pairs, and movement of the weight tends to be across the diagonal. It follows that it can only be corrected in trot. Hence, our straightness training is carried out mainly in trot.

As we said earlier, when a right-handed horse is working on the right rein, it relies on its right foreleg as its main support (see photo on p. 61; figs. on pp. 62 and 63; and review the text on p. 35). The outside (left) hind leg takes less than its share of the weight, and the right (diagonally opposite) foreleg takes more. This is a classic case of the weight (and thus, the center of gravity) moving diagonally forward from the left hip to the right shoulder. This results in the horse losing its balance. Too much weight is also thrown onto the inside hind leg, so that it cannot step forward properly, and cannot support the inside hindquarter or the inside shoulder as it should.

Diagonal Imbalance

The horse no longer steps under its center of gravity with its inside hindfoot. This results in a shortening of the arc traveled by the inside shoulder (see drawing on p. 45).

A right-handed horse (before correction) using its right foreleg as its main support.

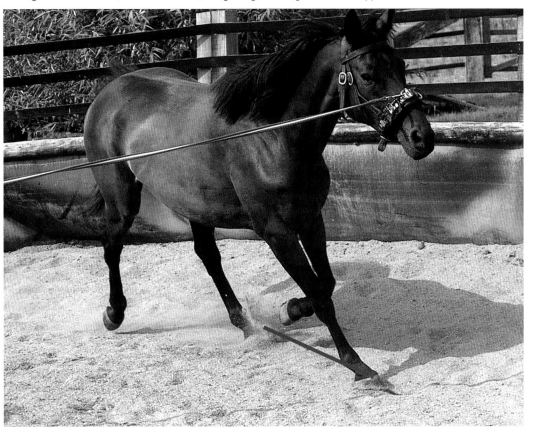

Illustrations on pp. 62 and 63: A crooked horse "putting its best foot forward" and placing extra weight on it: in a crooked horse the weight falls forward diagonally from the left hind foot onto the right forefoot. The only way to correct this is to shift the excess weight back across this diagnol.

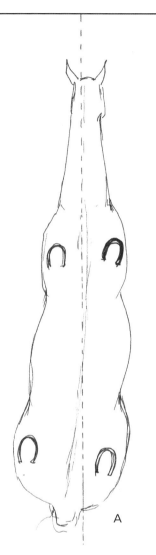

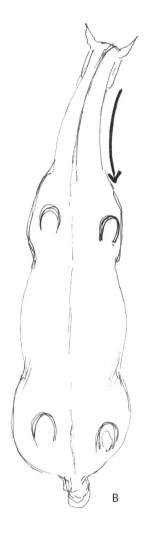

A

B

Natural crookedness causes a diagonal shift forward. Therefore, it can only be neutralized by a diagonal shift backward!

● *Natural crookedness in a right-handed or right-foreleg-dominant horse. Its weight is transferred diagonally forward onto the right shoulder, and so onto the right foreleg and forefoot (A).*

● *To correct this, ask the horse to bend its neck, which will cause the right shoulder to be drawn back (B).*

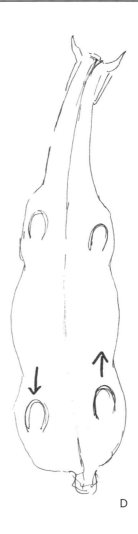

◉ At this point, the weight is transferred from the right shoulder diagonally backward to the left hindquarter (C).

◉ Only when this weight has been transferred to the outside hind leg can the inside hind leg step forward under the center of gravity and so support the right hindquarter, and at the same time lighten the right shoulder (D).

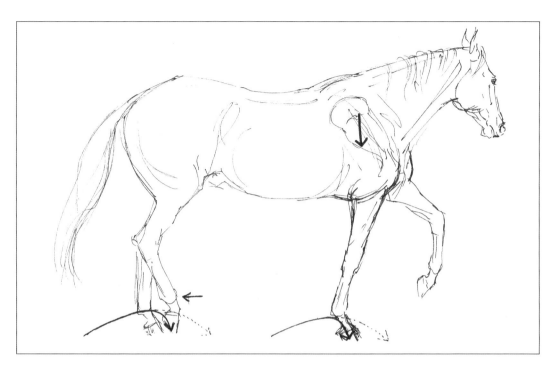

Here, the hind legs are taking "short-long-short" steps, causing the right shoulder to travel a shortened arc as shown in the drawing at the bottom of p. 45).

Over the course of time, the inside hind leg gradually shortens its step more and more, which of course slows the forward movement. The horse takes so-called "short-long-short" steps with its hind feet, i.e. shorter steps with one hind leg than the other.

It is obvious that this places a strain on the joints: As said earlier, *when the muscles can no longer cope, it is the bones that take the strain.*

Every horse reacts differently and in its own way to this diagonal imbalance, and effects are felt in all its gaits. These problems are a reflection of the horse's crookedness.

Before we leave this subject, we'd like to say a few words about cantering on the longe. As a rule, we do not work our horses in canter because we find it is very difficult to exercise control over what they are doing. This is because in canter as in trot, on the right rein a right-handed horse leans on its right shoulder, and swings its hindquarters out. On the left rein, it falls out with its right shoulder. This makes it difficult to ensure that the horse sets the outside hindfoot down first when we ask it to canter. Hence, we risk encouraging the horse to strike off onto the wrong canter lead. We find it is easier to work with horses in canter under saddle.

Correcting

Crookedness:

Practical Work

WHERE
TO TRAIN

The round pen or schooling ring

Centrifugal and *shear forces* are very difficult to control, and if they are not dealt with during basic training, they may cause problems later. Special attention needs to be paid to them. They are the first of the forces over which you must gain control, and you should do so even before the horse is ridden.

These forces will affect the ridden horse to an even greater extent when it is worked on turns and circles, so you must ensure that it will be able to cope. To remind you, the horse is a creature of flight and tends to want to move in a straight line, so it must learn to go round in a circle. If you work it in a normal rectangular school, the horse will find it harder to understand what we want it to do. Moreover, there will be nothing to restrict the centrifugal and shear forces, so these will be acting on it constantly. The logical solution is to construct a boundary: why not work in a place where it is as easy as possible for the horse to understand what is required of it? This is why we use a round pen, or circular schooling area.

A round pen, or circular school, 11 meters in diameter, which is our preferred size.

We are not the only ones to advocate a round pen. It is recommended in books about longeing including those of the FN (the German Equestrian Federation). Obviously, there are differing opinions on the size of the pen: for example the FN recommends a minimum diameter of 12 meters. However, the size depends on what you are using the pen for, so if it is for specialized corrective training the requirements are different. What suits one may not suit the other.

The fact that people are having so many problems with their horses, and that so many horses have to undergo corrective training, suggests that centrifugal and shear forces are the most difficult problems to deal with in training. To help you get to grips with these forces, we'll first set out a list of requirements as a guide. Without a proper framework, it is impossible to achieve your aim.

The first requirement is the round pen (or circular schooling area), which helps you with the difficult task of controlling these forces. We know from experience that 11 meters diameter is an ideal size for this pen.

Cavesson and longe line

Among the "tools of the trade" are the cavesson and longe line. Equipment has been the subject of much discussion, especially since the increase in popularity of different styles of riding, and in this case particularly the old style classical equitation. Our work is constantly being compared to this, that or the other, but there is no point spending time here discussing this. All we ask is that people do not judge our system by comparing us to others, but instead take the trouble to ask us why we are doing what we are doing. What is the background? This may take more effort but it is worth it. If you take your work seriously, as we do, you have your reasons for doing things. Here again we must ask people to be tolerant and open-minded.

We do not orientate our training toward any particular branch or style of horsemanship: we work with a specific aim in mind, namely correcting problems in the way of going that originate in incorrect training. The cavesson and longe line are there to help us achieve this aim. The style of riding and the job

EQUIPMENT

This type of longeing cavesson belongs only in the hands of professionals and experienced trainers.

This one, in our opinion, is the most suitable kind of cavesson for the average rider. Experience shows that because of its fit and its precise action, it is "kind" to the horse.

the horse has to do are not important.

We like both models of cavesson shown in the photos above. This is because they fit the horse's head exactly, with the noseband just below the cheekbone. A cavesson must not slip because it needs to be precise in its action: close control over the horse's longitudinal axis is crucial to the success of training. The cavesson in the first photo is a modified design with a very precise action. It is the "professional" model, which means that its use requires more skill. Since it has no browband or throatlatch, it enables the horse to be controlled with a lighter contact and is less bulky and more comfortable than the second shown cavesson. It is important that the part of the noseband around the nasal bone is particularly well-padded. The second cavesson is excellent for use by amateurs.

How the cavesson should fit

When fitting the cavesson, it is important to bear in mind how it works. You can only achieve correct lateral bend when the action is clear and precise. However, this is only possible when the cavesson fits snugly and there is nothing to irritate the horse and so provoke resistance. The noseband should fit securely, a finger's width below the bottom of the cheekbone, where it is fastened around a very stable and relatively insensitive part of the horse's head. The cheek strap should also be fastened securely to prevent the cheek piece pulling up and rubbing the eye. The throatlatch should be slack.

For all our straightness training, the longe rein should be attached to the middle ring on the noseband. We do not use the two outer rings, which are for attaching side reins. Side reins play no part in our training.

The small rings on the cheek pieces are for attaching a bit during certain phases of longe work—especially when training driving horses.

How the cavesson works

Before going on to discuss how the cavesson works, one further point must be mentioned. We are often asked whether the horse can also be longed in a halter (US) or headcollar (UK). Our answer to this is a definite "no"! Firstly, a halter (headcollar) fits very loosely on the horse's head and would move about. Secondly, the action of the longe line would be acting on the side (not the front) of the horse's head, making it impossible to bend the horse in its body.

As just mentioned, you should also avoid longeing with side reins, since they interfere with the trainer's "feel." Moreover, if the horse is wearing side reins, you have no control or influence over the all-important center of gravity and the crookedness (see photo, p. 70). Here again, the basic principle applies: the horse cannot learn what is required if it cannot be shown how to do it, or is physically prevented from doing so.

At this point, you need to backtrack and remind yourself of the function of the *longissimus* muscle (pp. 24 and 25). You have seen that you need to control the horse's body through-

⚙ *Here, the bend in the horse's neck is clearly visible, free from the restriction of side reins.*

⚙ *When viewed from above, the longe line forms a 90-degree angle with the horse's head and neck.*

out its length—from the head to the hindquarters. The longe rein is the connection between you, the trainer, and the front end of the horse's longitudinal axis. During straightness training, nothing must interfere with this connection, that is, with the action of the longe rein. This applies particularly to side reins, which tend to lock the horse in its "front-heavy," crooked position rather than help to change it.

There are many ways, both good and bad, to work a horse on the longe, so we must explain how you should go about it. Firstly, if you were to view from above the horse's head should always be at an angle of 90 degrees to the longe line. This is the only way you can bend the neck and the longitudinal axis accurately.

What is the basis of our longe training? Once again, it is the *longissimus* muscle that is involved because it is the only one to run the whole length of the horse's longitudinal axis. The third in its list of functions, as mentioned earlier, is lateral bend. We make use of this muscle's sideways-bending capability to counteract another of its functions—putting weight onto the forehand.

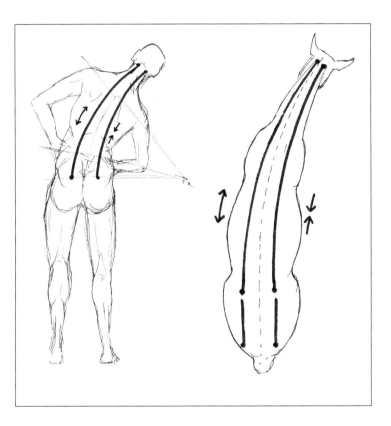

● The part played by the longissimus muscle in lateral flexion.

● The head and neck turned to the outside (wrong bend) in a right-handed horse turning to the right (A). When its neck is correctly bent to the right instead, the horse starts to work through its back and move its right shoulder freely (B).

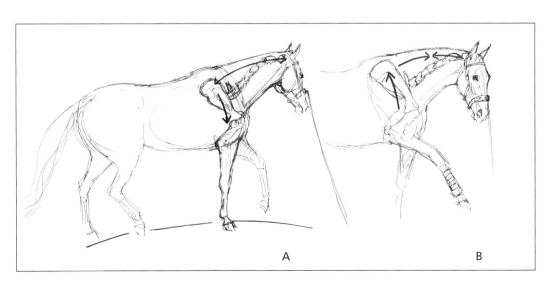

A   B

Since tension develops first in the neck area, the first stage in work on the longe consists of suppling the neck. The aim is to be able to control the shoulders. As we have already said, only if the horse is working through its shoulders can the forces that have such a negative effect on training—centrifugal and shear—be brought under control. Only if the neck is free from tension and "lets your aids through" can you influence the shoulders. This is crucial and must be kept in mind at all times. Hence it follows that:

Control over the shoulders = control over the diagonal*
(*the diagonal transfer of weight from right shoulder
back toward the outside hind leg)

This is where a well-fitting cavesson comes in. We used to think it should be of a certain weight, but we now consider this to be of secondary importance.

The "shoulder stick"

It is often helpful to use a "shoulder stick" (or "training stick") as an auxiliary aid in straightness training on the longe (www. naturalhorsesupply.com). With many horses, bending on its own is not enough to get to grips with crookedness, and using a shoulder stick at the same time is very effective. Use it just behind the shoulder joint (see photos on p. 74). If applied at

A shoulder stick.

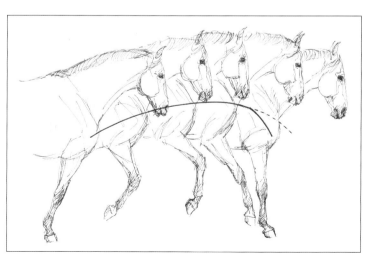

the same time that the neck is being bent by the action of the cavesson and longe, it prevents the horse shortening the arc traveled by its shoulder and so putting its foot down prematurely, as is happening in the drawing on p. 72.

It then also becomes easier to get the horse to transfer its weight diagonally from the right shoulder backward toward the outside hind leg (see photos below and on p. 74).

The whip

For this longeing, we use a carriage-driving whip, because it makes it easier to act directly on the shoulders. We avoid driving the hindquarters forward, since in early training this only serves to increase the "sideways" forces, shear and centrifugal. However, once the horse is established in self-carriage, this is rarely a problem.

🔘 *Longeing a right-handed horse with the carriage-driving whip that we prefer, but not using the shoulder stick here. See the next page for two photos demonstrating use of the shoulder stick.*

The shoulder stick being used properly in two different phases of movement.

LONGEING

"Pecking order" and dominance

Before beginning to explain our system of straightness training through longeing, we'll discuss a few introductory points.

In our experience, the urge to become herd leader seems to be genetically programmed into animals. The position in the pecking order depends, among other things, on the animal's physical capabilities, such as speed, agility and athleticism. These, in turn, are dependent on the position of the horse's center of gravity, since the better the horse's balance, the faster, more agile and more athletic it is. Taking this one step further, we can say that the *straighter* the horse is, the faster, more agile and more athletic it is, also.

If you are to get to grips with the problems that arise during the course of the straightness training, you need to learn to put yourself in the horse's place: to "feel as the horse feels." You must allow the horse to do what comes naturally, that is, to find its place in the "horse and man" herd.

It is relatively easy to establish a pecking order in an enclosed space such as a round pen. It is also easier in this "mini-herd" to teach the horse the rules of the game. The pecking order, and the dominance of the trainer, must be made clear to the horse. It is a known fact that a horse that is integrated in the herd—that is, a horse that "knows its place"—is also mentally well-balanced. This is important for all training that lies ahead. As the dominant being, you take on the responsibility for teaching the horse speed, agility and athleticism.

The trainer makes the horse straight!

This training teaches the horse self-confidence, and helps it to gain a sense of identity. It also develops its capacity for responding to pressure.

Unfortunately, all too often we see horses whose behavior is characterized by cowed submission. The training of these horses reflects an unfortunate side of human nature: obedience has been obtained by force. This has nothing to do with normal social behavior of herd animals. No herd leader uses his position to subjugate those below him in the pecking order. It must surely be ignorance, in most cases, that causes people to go to these extremes.

While on the subject of ignorance, an aside: another example of lack of understanding is something we often hear our customers say, namely: "Don't make him too strong in his back, or he will be more difficult to train." What a thing to say! And another example: we'd like to tell a little story that we wrote down in a notebook a long time ago about the meaning of the term "horsemanship." Imagine a wide river with a bridge over it. People live on one side, and horses on the other. Someone goes over the bridge, gets a horse, takes it back with him across to the people's side of the bridge and tries to ride it, but runs into problems. Someone else goes over the bridge, and gets the horse used to being ridden on its side of the river before taking it across the bridge away from its familiar environment. No problem! It is the second rider who is the true horseman. Sometimes we can learn from stories such as these.

Now back to the straightness work on the longe. What is the best way to go about explaining it? The simplest way is to describe what we actually do every day. The horses stay with us at the Center for three weeks and we work them on the longe every day, except Mondays. The first stage of their training is then complete. When they come to us they are affected by a variety of different physical and mental problems, which we have already explained, and which made them unusable. After the three weeks of training they are ready to be taken over by their rider again. As we said before, this is the beginning of a difficult time for the rider. He must learn how to learn from his horse! He is getting on a horse that, three weeks later, has been correctly trained, and moving much more freely and correctly. The rider does not yet know what to do, and is given strict instructions. It looked easy when we were demonstrating, but he finds it very difficult. He needs to be able to focus his full attention on the horse's movement. Every rider at the Center must watch and feel his horse and learn from it.

After three weeks, the horse's crookedness (that is, its right- or left-handedness) is controllable, and the rider should be able to keep it this way. If he takes the trouble, he should even be able to bring about further improvement. The rider's biggest problem at this point is fear of making mistakes. This is understandable, since when he brought the horse to us he thought that its problems were his fault. This was not strictly true, or at least he cannot take sole responsibility. He does not want to make any more mistakes, and, of course, this in itself holds up progress. This is where he needs our help. He must learn that he is allowed to make mistakes. We often find that riders expect themselves to be perfect straightaway. We have to tell them to be patient. First, they must learn and feel, and above all develop self-confidence. They must reach the stage where they can ride the horse correctly at the Center, but above all, can continue to do so when they get home. What we must remember is that the horse's problems have been solved, but its home environment has not changed. Care must be taken not to fall straight back into the old ways upon return.

You must ask yourself two questions when you start working a horse on the longe:
1. Why are you longeing the horse in this way?
2. What are you trying to achieve with this work?

To ensure that things are done correctly, at this point we must repeat that you need to keep the "big picture" in mind and make sure that what you are doing is in context.

The answer to the first question is very important, since it explains the difference between *normal* and *corrective* training on the longe. These two forms of longeing are completely different in their approaches and aims. As you now know, centrifugal and shear forces are caused by crookedness and originate in the forehand. You can also see that, if these forces are not quickly brought under control, the consequences can be disastrous.

As touched on earlier, by acting on, and exercising control over the shoulders you can dramatically reduce these forces, and eventually make them controllable. The crookedness, and with it the movement of the weight diagonally forward from the hip to the opposite shoulder, is reduced to a minimum, which relieves the heaviness on the forehand. All this is done before you even get on the horse's back. This is why we do our corrective longe work in this way!

The answer to the second question is that we do this longe work with one aim in mind: to produce a horse that moves with its hindquarters aligned with its forehand, who works forward and downward through an "*upward*-swinging back." This is nothing new, but simply what every rider is trying to achieve with his horse. Unfortunately though, until now he has not usually managed it: in 80 percent of the horses the back does not swing upward. So we need to make the point again, even more emphatically. There are numerous reasons why the horse's back needs to swing upward: we have already discussed them (see p. 30), and they cannot be repeated too often. Because of the way the *longissimus* muscle works, if the back "swings" downward, the horse's weight goes *onto its forehand*.

Moreover, it needs to be understood that when the back swings downward, that is, the downward bend is greater than the upward bend, it means that the horse is not in balance and is tending to run after, or "chase" its center of gravity, which drives its weight even more forward and onto one shoulder. It is therefore impossible for the horse to develop rhythm and impulsion, and above all to work through its back.

Technical considerations

Now we come to the technical details of our straightness training. We have already mentioned the potential difficulties of this work. We have also pointed out that it is dangerous for people who have not previously worked with this system to start off by trying it out on a problem horse. This applies particularly to riders who lack the experience to recognize and understand where and how the crookedness is affecting their horse. We must also emphasize that horses are widely differing individuals, and that implementation of the technique must vary from horse to horse, so the progression we are about to describe may well be unsuitable for your horse. We are very cautious about giving exact lists of instructions. We take a great deal of time and trouble over our training, which is why it cannot be condensed into a set formula. We take this trouble because it is our duty to the horse as a living creature, and this is also why we try to get riders to learn about their horses.

First, you need to know what type of horse you are dealing with: not just its breed, but whether the horse is right- or left-handed. This is important because it sets the stage for the work ahead.

Everyone who has had a problem riding a small circle needs to understand that the horse will tend to make the circle bigger or smaller depending on the direction and on the side of its dominant front foot. Note that when the horse makes the circle smaller, the centrifugal force increases. It follows that the causes of centrifugal force can be traced back to the horse's right- or left-handedness: it lies dormant, as it were, and is triggered as soon as the horse starts to move. It must be eliminated, and this is achieved through straightness training. It is no use trying to explain away movement problems due to the effects of centrifugal force by making the excuse that the circle is too small. You must simply face up to the problem and set about correcting it as quickly as possible.

Straightness training

To remind you, we will discuss everything in relation to a *right-handed* horse. As a general rule, we do not *start* working such a horse to the *right*. This direction is its "stress side" because of the shear forces involved, which come into action only when the right-handed horse is turning to the right. (See p. 43 for more explanation.)

Starting the longeing to the left, the first aim is to get yourself into the position of being able to exercise control over the shoulders. This is essential. Start by "asking" the horse to yield in its neck and bend it to the left. What do we mean by "asking"? There is a natural tendency, if something does not work straight away, to apply more pressure. In this case, this would mean pulling, which would be totally wrong since it would trigger an opposite reaction in the horse. The more you pull, the more the horse will pull back, which does nothing to advance the cause! This is why we specify "asking" the horse to yield in its neck. This can also be described as "Tighten, immediately release; repeat." These intermittent signals give the horse's muscles no chance to tense and set up a counter-reaction. The result is that the horse yields in its neck.

People often make the big mistake in this situation of setting their shoulders against the horse. (You can test to see if you do this while sitting on the horse. Almost all riders, including some professionals, sit with their shoulders stiff or rigid. This automatically causes the hands to stiffen. The horse notices this immediately, and a counter-reaction develops slowly but surely.) Longeing provides a good opportunity to study and eliminate this reaction. This needs to be done as soon as possible, otherwise problems develop unnecessarily that may disguise other faults.

What the horse does with its hindquarters is not important at this stage, since you'll only be able to do something about these when you can influence the horse appropriately through the relevant shoulder.

On this left rein, you'll have the impression that there is a very strong sideways pull on the neck. The *longissimus* muscle is under tension as a result of *centrifugal force*, which, to remind you, acts on the right-handed horse when it is working on the *left rein*. The horse becomes concave to the *left*. This seems complicated, but all will become clear once the explanations so far have been mastered.

Now to longeing in the other direction, on the right rein. Here, you have the problem that the horse uses its *right* foreleg to brace itself. Usually, the head goes up at the same time. Why? Low shoulder equals high head. The horse tries to relieve the weight on the right shoulder by "steering away" from it, that is, carrying its head to the outside. You must remember: *the neck is the horse's rudder.*

You can see that the early stages of work on the right rein

A right-handed horse being asked to bend to the left. This horse had not yet begun its corrective training. The result: it is falling out through its outside shoulder. Note the direction the outside hind leg is about to go—toward the ouside of the ring. This is caused by centrifugal force.

require skill on the part of the person who is longeing. As when you longe on the left rein ignore the reaction of the hindquarters at the start. Of course, you should expect improvement as work progresses. As explained earlier, a horse loses its balance by falling onto or out through its shoulders, and to control it you need to influence or work through the shoulders. Consequently, you need to remain constantly in the shoulder area when longeing (see photos demonstrating this on p. 82). However, since the horse is moving, and the shoulders are following a circular track, you have to learn to keep pace with its movement. You must keep moving, and stay level with its shoulder. This may seem strange, at first, because it is probably different from the longeing method you are used to, but that gives no control over the horse's shoulders. However, you need this control to tackle the centrifugal and shear forces that are generated.

◑ The same right-handed horse as pictured on p. 80 being asked to bend to the right. Result: as a consequence of shear forces, it is leaning on its inside foreleg, its head has gone up, and its body is trying to veer to the left. The left hind leg is bracing against the shear forces.

A sequence of corrective longeing positions

The "driving" position.

The "accompanying" position.

The "maintaining" position.

The "active" position prior to halting.

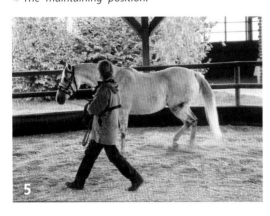

The "preparing" position prior to halting.

In this position the horse comes to a halt.

In order to remain level with the horse's shoulders, you have to move quite energetically to stay "with" the horse. Your action with the longe line itself should consist of a series of short impulses, which are transmitted via the cavesson to the nose, that is, to the front end of the longitudinal axis (*longissimus* muscle). The result is that the horse will yield in its neck, which is its rudder, allowing you to begin to exercise control over the shoulders. The heaviness in front and crookedness will then gradually disappear.

The excess weight is then moved backward diagonally from the inside right shoulder toward the outside left hind leg, allowing the horse to step with its inside hindfoot forward under its center of gravity. Centrifugal and shear forces subside. The horse finds its balance and begins to work through its back. The weight of the body is carried by the hindquarters, so the horse no longer needs to compensate for its lack of balance by turning its head and neck outward. Rhythm and impulsion become easy.

Reviewing tack

At our Center, when we reach the point where the rider learns to longe his horse, we take time to review the horse's tack. The horse has become stronger in its back and the muscles around the withers and in the upward-swinging part of the back—where the saddle rests—have become more developed. So it is unlikely a saddle that *may* have fit before will still fit now that the horse is working correctly through its back.

We use the expression "may have fit" on purpose, because in our experience, most saddles did not fit in the first place! In any case, whether it did or not, when we place the saddle on the horse at this point in its training, it is difficult to imagine that it ever fit properly.

We are very careful with our choice of a new saddle. We avoid certain types because we have found that they do not withstand the pressures of an upward-swinging back.

As to the flock, suffice it to say that for a horse with an upward-swinging back, you do not need excessively deep padding. Too much, or possibly too hard stuffing, in conjunction with the weight of the rider, will restrict the upward swing and curve of the horse's back. A saddle with a thin layer of soft stuffing allows the rider to feel the horse. The saddle is then doing its job: it is helping horse and rider to work together.

The rider will then be able to feel his horse's reaction to being ridden again for the first time after its corrective training. This is very important, since the rider must be able to recognize and interpret the signals that the horse sends out.

So we have now reached the point where you can get on your horse. How much has the horse changed during its corrective training? To be able to feel and judge this, you should first try to improve and train your seat by doing riding exercises while being longed by someone else.

How to feel the seat bones.

Longeing

A rider experiencing how the horse feels after its training and doing some exercises to develop an independent seat (see text on p. 86).

THE RIDER'S SEAT

Information on how to sit can be found in various specialist books on the subject, and more and more courses are being offered for training the rider's seat. Yet again and again, we are confronted with rider problems. These take two forms: how to sit, and how to use your body to influence the horse.

The seat is affected by the horse's way of going. A horse that is on its forehand, that is, heavy in front, and consequently "swinging downward" with its back, is difficult or almost impossible to sit.

If the horse is unbalanced, you will also be unable to find your balance.

As mentioned earlier, when, after three weeks of preparation and corrective training on the longe, we put the rider on the horse again, it is always a moment of revelation for him. Typically, we hear, "This is not the same horse. I have never been able to sit him like this before." This may be partly due to the fact that during his previous training the rider had been given little or no information about sitting correctly and in balance. We have now achieved the first, very important objective of our training: the horse is basically in balance, and ready and able to carry the rider's weight, and in a position to do so. The horse now swings upward with its back and takes you with it. You can let yourself move with the horse without disturbing it.

In this connection, we'll explain once again how you should position your body from an "anatomical" point of view so you can sit without actively using your muscles—without using strength.

In man, as in the horse, the abdominal muscles are the direct antagonists of the back muscles. Since man walks and moves in an upright position, he can actively and consciously control his abdominal muscles. This allows him to establish a correct seat—on his *two seat bones* and *perineum*—by stabilizing his two dorsal extensor muscles. In contrast to the opinion commonly held—even in scientific circles—that the three support points should be the two seat bones and *pubic bone*, we recommend a three-point seat based on the seat bones and perineum. We have found in our experience of correcting the way people sit that the pubic bone is too close to the vagina or testicles.

We have also found that many people are in pain when they

ride, which is wrong. Unfortunately, soreness is a subject that is still rarely discussed, with both men and women preferring to suffer in silence. We are of the same opinion as the nineteenth century riding master, Gustav Steinbrecht, who even in those days scoffed at the idea of forcing the rider into a prescribed position before he was used to the feeling of his body on the horse. Furthermore, we do not advocate riding without stirrups to improve the rider's seat. It invariably leads to riding "on the fork" and then to "clinging on" with the legs.

When you have learned to use the pelvis and pelvic floor muscles to "rock" the pelvis, you are in a position to "go with" the upward swinging of the horse's back. To understand what we mean by "rocking" the pelvis, sit on a chair, a simple kitchen chair for example, with your seat bones on the front edge of the chair, and tilt the chair onto its front legs by tightening your stomach muscles. Keep on doing it until it comes easily to you. This is what you do when you move with the upward-swinging movement of the horse's back.

When you first start doing this you will become very aware of, that is, be able to "feel" your abdominal muscles, and maybe also the tightening of your inner thigh muscles. But soreness and backache will be a thing of the past. The straight line through shoulder, hip and heel is obtained easily through these exercises, and without creating tension. Your heels flex downward naturally, without needing to be forced down by bending the ankle. You are now also in balance. You "intermesh" with the horse's movement like a gear wheel. Your legs and hands are now still.

Riding your horse in its now "changed" state, after its straightness training, you need to become established in this new position, and learn to feel whether you are moving "with" or "against" the horse's movement—its rhythm. For your seat to be independent, you need to be able to find and keep your balance, which means that these exercises should always take place on the longe, using a cavesson. Riders, even professionals, often find it frustrating that without reins they can hardly sit on the horse at all. We train the rider to use his hips to enable him to stay "with" the horse so that his upper body can remain independent and not disturb the horse's rhythm. The rider's center of gravity then moves to the center of his body, with the result that his shoulder area becomes independent and free, as then do his hands.

In riding, the correct use of the back consists of tightening the back muscles in conjunction with your pelvis and pelvic floor muscles as described above, and coordinating the action of these two opposing sets of muscles. This is what is commonly, but misleadingly, referred to as "bracing the back."

Having dealt with rider "technique," we'll now come back to our system and the next stage in the process. The first lessons with the bit and reins should take place in a round pen or similar area so as to establish these new experiences in the mind of horse and rider.

When you first get on (see *Transition from Work on the Ground to Work under Saddle* on p. 90), you will still clearly feel the difference between your horse's left and right side. Though it may not seem logical, the crookedness will have reasserted itself now that the horse has your weight on its back. In fact, this is a very important part of straightness training, namely the transition from work on the ground to work under saddle. This is when the horse's reaction to your weight enters the equation. However, since the horse has been prepared from the ground, it is now relatively easy to explain to it how to carry a rider. This is where your ability to "feel" comes in and this is the reason for your doing exercises to train your seat.

You will be able to feel, if you do not intervene, that your right-handed horse will move with considerably more impulsion on the left rein than it does on the right (the side of the dominant forelimb). What does this mean for the rider? You must remain straight, and not allow yourself to be "twisted" or "pulled out of shape" by your horse. It is very important also, on the right rein, to allow your left (outside) leg to drop down until you can feel your right seat bone. You are then "square" to the horse: the lines of communication between horse and rider are open! It is here that the age-old maxim that the rider's shoulders should be parallel to the horse's shoulders takes on its full meaning, since you need to be in this position to get the horse to take the weight off its right shoulder. The weight must be transferred to the horse's outside hind leg. At some point, you may say, "I'm sitting all crooked and against the horse," since the horse is still crooked because of the addition of your weight. It is now up to you to sort out the problem by using the longeing system of corrective training to teach the horse to be straight.

Generally we estimate that a period of about three months is needed for horse and rider to "come together." This may seem a long time, but our aim is to make the rider independent so that he can cope on his own. We help him with the "general application" of straightness training through the longe—and ridden work. It is then up to him to apply all this afterward to his particular sport.

Our main aim at our Center is to correct crookedness in horses of all ages. Horses have developed problems because mistakes have been made when riding or training them. The reasons for the problems have been described earlier. Some of these horses have even been given up as a "bad job" by professionals. We are proud to have succeeded with these horses, but it also leaves us with a feeling of sadness.

We feel that many horses are needlessly destroyed because their owners do not understand the significance of crookedness. Many people who have just bought a young, unbroken horse, and who have perhaps had a bad experience with their last horse, ask if we recommend our straightness training for young, unbroken horses, and how we go about it in such cases. When horses—and people—come into the world, they do not immediately show recognizable signs of right- or left-handedness, that is, limb dominance or laterality (favoring one side over the other). This is something that develops in the early stages of their life. It is when the "playing stage" gets underway that the first clear signs appear whether the young horse is right- or left-handed. At the same time, visible evidence of shear and centrifugal forces show up. These forces affect all horses: the horse grows up with them. However, it is still worth considering just how these forces affect the young horse.

Some of these effects have already been discussed. The biggest problems, however, arise when not enough time is spent on the horse's training, as often happens, especially in the case of talented horses. The horse should be given the *first stage* of straightness training at the age of two-and-a-half to three

THE

YOUNG

HORSE

years. This is not "work": it is simply training aimed at teaching the horse how to use its body. Being able to move faster and more confidently will make it easier for the horse to perform the exercises required of it later in its training. If this training is then followed up with further work on the longe until such time as the horse is backed, it will have benefited from one to two years preparation (depending on the age at which it is first ridden). Horses trained in this way present few problems later.

With a young, unridden horse, after a month of straightness training we put it back out with the other horses. That is its *first stage*. Loose in the field, while playing, it is practicing what it has learned. A year to 18 months later, the *second stage* of training begins consisting of further correction of balance and then—very importantly—*familiarization* with sights and sounds. All this takes place before the horse's first encounter with the saddle. If the young horse is prepared in this way it will have no problem when the saddle is put on its back for the first time. It will still be on the longe line, which it is used to, and it trusts its handler implicitly so it will not mind, even, when someone gets on its back.

TRANSITION FROM WORK ON THE GROUND TO WORK UNDER SADDLE

When preparing to back the horse for the first time, you should always stand on something to raise yourself above ground level. You will not have so far to go to get into the saddle and will avoid pulling the saddle sideways.

The *third stage* consists in riding the horse in walk, trot and canter. You should finish up with a horse that does not mind whatever it is asked to do; stress should not be part of its vocabulary. It is at ease with its rider.

One more point that should be taken into consideration: the horse's bones are not hard enough to be stressed to the maximum until it is about five years old. So, if you are trying to produce the horse in the shortest possible time, as mentioned above, you at least owe it to do everything possible to protect it from harm. You should, therefore, train it to be straight before you get on it for the first time. Have the courage to do as much as possible of the straightness training from the ground even if people keep telling you that you should do it from the saddle.

All the practices recommended from now on belong in the category of ridden training. They are the application of the corrective training. These are practices aimed at making the horse better able to carry the rider, and increasing its performance capability by influencing the forehand and center of gravity. They serve to set rider and horse on the road to success. It must be stressed that they are not at variance with classical principles: they are simply a detour that leads back to the road to success.

We start with a stress-free horse ready to go on to its training under saddle. Elements of the corrective training that dominated the longe work, in particular the *control of the shoulders*, must be incorporated in the work under saddle.

First of all, we must mention the concept of the "support leg" and the "free leg," even if it is not usually discussed in connection with horses. To understand it, you need to look at human anatomy and behavior. In a right-handed person, the left leg is the support leg, and consequently, the right leg is the free leg.

However, drawing your right shoulder forward blocks the movement of the free leg. The weight is no longer concentrated on the support leg, and your inside leg can no longer step forward.

A person standing on his "support leg." The right "free leg" can be drawn forward to kick the ball. In order to lift this leg, the shoulder on the same side must be drawn back.

Bringing the right shoulder forward blocks movement of the "free leg." Compare these drawings with the horse on p. 92.

How does this work in the case of the horse? First, we must point out that man and horse react in almost identical ways with their bodies. This can be seen particularly in situations where man cannot use his more highly developed brain, for example, in stress situations such as a fall, or simply if he stands on all fours, that is, if he adopts a horizontal position.

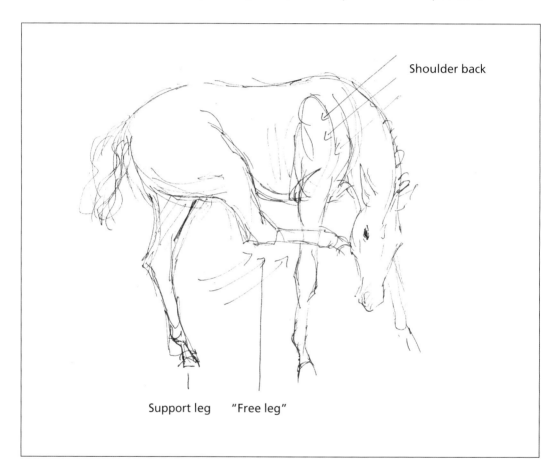

Shoulder back

Support leg   "Free leg"

Compare this to the drawings of the human on p. 91. Here is similar use of the "support leg" and "free leg" in the horse.

If a person is standing with his shoulder forward, when he drops onto all fours that shoulder will be lower. The horse, which lives on all fours, displays similar behavior.

Understanding your own body's reaction will make it easier for you to relate to what your horse is doing. So when the horse's right shoulder is lower than its left, the action of the inside hind leg (free leg) is blocked, and the outside hind leg (support leg) does not take its share of the weight.

In a right-handed horse the left hind leg is the support leg, and always will be so long as the horse remains crooked. Let us explain this further: in a right-handed horse the left hind leg is its natural "support leg," and the right hind leg is its "free leg." We have explained earlier how the weight is tipped diagonally forward onto the inside shoulder. This causes a shortening of the arc traveled by the inside shoulder, and blocks the movement of the inside hind leg.

Once again: we must accept that a crooked horse, a horse that has not been trained to be straight, will remain like this indefinitely. A right-handed horse working on the right rein will always block the movement of its inside hind leg by lowering and leaning on its right shoulder. This happens every time the horse is ridden, and continues until the rider has had enough or the horse starts to resist.

It therefore follows: *the horse cannot be said to be straight unless it can swap its support leg and free leg (the outside hind leg should always be the support leg) when it changes from the right to the left rein and back again.* If the horse cannot do so, serious rhythm faults are one likely consequence.

This is a good time to reflect on the significance of the different figures or exercises that we perform every day while under instruction and as part of our everyday work with the horse. The riders who come to us notice immediately, with surprise, that they are asked to do things differently, and cannot understand why. One example is a "serpentine across the width of the school." In this exercise, every change of rein over the centerline is an excellent opportunity to transfer the weight onto the new outside hind leg—the support leg—by changing the flexion and lifting the new inside shoulder. This is an excellent test of whether the horse is working through its back, as well as its ability to swap its support leg and free leg. This exercise also increases the engagement and activity of the hindquarters. Unfortunately, however, in the "modern" serpentine the part between the curves has been straightened out: instead of looping back on itself, the horse now goes straight across the center. This means that much of the value of this figure as a suppling exercise has been lost, which is a pity.

Every rider should watch dressage tests being performed

PREPARING THE HORSE FOR FUTURE WORK

and ask himself where the main visible difficulties lie. We are convinced that they are often caused by riding the horse forward "at all costs." *We must ride forward, this is indisputable, but not with the horse leaning on the dominant forelimb.*

As a result of the corrective training on the longe, your horse is well prepared for ridden work. It must be clearly understood that the longe work is only the first stage. In this next stage, the horse needs to be helped to learn to cope with its right- or left-handedness with the weight of the rider on its back. The word "helped" has been carefully chosen. Since, as upright beings, we have a better understanding of what it means to be vertical, we can communicate to the horse what is required, though to do this we also need to understand what it means to be straight and in balance with the horse. This is an important point that we'll look at in more detail.

Obtain freedom and looseness

Freedom and looseness is obtained by releasing muscle tension. It is the *first stage* in the ridden work and is, so to speak, compulsory. Riding the horse "forward and downward" belongs in this phase, so lowering the head and neck is an essential requirement.

However, you need to remember and take into account how the horse behaved during its training on the longe. As a right-handed horse, it made the circle smaller on the right rein and bigger on the left rein. You learned that the behavior of the shoulders leads to the development of shear and centrifugal forces, and that these cause problems in future training if not brought under control. We know that getting the horse to work with freedom and looseness depends on it being in balance. If, on the longe, you achieved this by exercising control over the appropriate shoulder, you must now do the same in the ridden work.

The success of the "loosening" phase depends on the tact and "feel" of the rider. Simply driving the horse relentlessly forward and downward will not get rid of the tension and get the horse to swing through its back.

Let us look at looseness from another angle. If you can understand that the horse loses its balance onto or out through its shoulder, you'll realize that muscle tension is also involved here. You must stop the horse falling out through its shoulder because *you cannot get it to relax its muscles if it is crooked.*

Crookedness is easiest to observe (and correct) on a curved track—a circle, for example. The work on the longe in a round pen was the first part of this system of training: it prepared the horse for the ridden work on the circle, which in its turn is part of the transition from the work on the ground to the work under saddle. Rider and horse now need to use the whole arena for the rest of the loosening-up work.

The horse will only begin to swing through its back when it is no longer falling out through, or leaning on its shoulder.

None of this work should be difficult, since the horse has been taught to balance itself during the corrective training. It already knows how to move through its back. Your task is simply to help the horse do—with your weight on its back—what it has already learned to do without a rider. You must use tact and "horse sense" to prevent the horse from falling out through its shoulder and to get it to swing through its back. It is during this phase of the preparation that the horse develops "tautness," that is, body-tightness or gymnastic tension. However, if it is simply driven relentlessly forward and downward, as time goes on, negative tension will develop, which will prevent it from developing the correct tautness. You need to clearly understand the difference between tautness and negative tension.

We hope it is clear by now why, in *Straightness Training* (p. 79) we started by working the right-handed horse on circles to the *left*, and then to the right. Remember: on the left rein, the centrifugal force causes the horse to fall out through its shoulder. On the right rein, the horse leans or "braces" itself on its right shoulder and foreleg and shear forces come into play.

You now understand this, so you can apply what you've learned to ridden work. To start with, you need to work differently with the horse on the right rein than on the left. You do this as a means to an end. It is a transitional stage. Whatever you use to help you at this stage, including your aids for example, is transient and is aimed simply at getting the horse to move freely and in balance.

The horse's reaction time

It is very important that you understand how fast the horse reacts. Its reaction time is much shorter than ours. With the horse we are dealing with a reaction speed of 0.4 seconds in "danger" situations. This is something we need to think about. Since we are inferior to the horse in this respect, we have to compensate by using our superior intellectual ability.

We also need to use our "horse sense." What do we mean by this? Two things are important here: we know from our experience that horses always react in the same way when we ride in certain places. What tends to happen is that the rider also keeps doing the same thing at that same place. However, because of the horse's reaction speed, the rider's response will always be too late. As a result, there is a "disagreement," and the rider often ends up using strength to try to control the horse. Obviously, the only way to prevent this scene being enacted is to "anticipate" what the horse is about to do. If we know when and where the horse is going to "act up," we can begin to perform appropriate exercises a few meters beforehand.

For example, when you ride a right-handed horse on a circle to the left, every time you turn away from the wall, through the center of the school, the horse falls out through its right shoulder, making the circle bigger. You have probably been trying to counteract this through the use of your outside rein and outside leg. And, have used these aids more strongly each time, but to very little effect. This is because they have come too late. Instead, you need to start to flex the horse to the outside three to four meters before turning away from the wall. By acting sooner, you are making it impossible for the horse to fall out. Rather than getting stronger and stronger, the aids can then be gradually refined as the horse becomes more sensitive to their use. Frequent use can be made of this technique during the horse's training. If you leave things too late, the horse will take advantage!

Riding a right-handed horse on the right rein

You now know that if the horse has not been straightened, it places excess weight or leans on its right shoulder and foreleg when on the right rein. By so doing it restricts the action of its inside hind leg and takes the weight off the outside hind leg (the weight moves forward across the diagonal to the inside shoulder). Its hindquarters, pivoting around the inside foreleg, "shear away" to the outside, resulting in a lowering of the inside hip. The head and neck point to the outside. You also know that through corrective straightness training, all these problems can be solved. However, all right-handed horses—and indeed all mammals—possess a "muscle-memory" reflex, which causes them to do things as they did them before. When you first get on your horse after its corrective training, this reflex will "kick in." The horse needs your help. You must act clearly and positively to prevent it reappearing.

You first need to focus all your attention on lightening the horse's right shoulder. Place your weight on your right seat bone and draw back your right shoulder, which lengthens your outside leg (see photo on p. 98). To put it another way, as your weight gets transferred onto your right seat bone, your center of

The rider's weight is on the right seat bone. His left heel is under his center of gravity. The right knee is pressed against the horse's right shoulder. The rider draws his right shoulder back. With his right hand he brings the right rein toward the right side of his chest, thus "lifting" the horse's right shoulder and extending the arc traveled by it.

Doing the exercise shown in the drawing on p. 97: a right-handed horse on the right rein. Notice the reins remain parallel to the shoulders. The rider, Doris Schwab, could bring her right shoulder back more.

gravity moves backward and to the left, and the horse's rib cage arches outward coming into contact with your left leg. Bring your right rein upward toward the chest. Pay special attention in this exercise to weight and balance, that is, the position of your center of gravity.

With respect to this exercise, a few important observations need to be made at this point. You are probably thinking, "I can't ride like this," or "I can't ride in a competition like this." Correct! No one ever said that you should—remember that it is a means to an end!

For the moment, you should consciously ride this way in order to help the horse understand. This is different from how you usually ride. As we've just said, the end justifies the means. Do not place your weight on your inside (right) stirrup, as you may have been taught to do. This is counter-productive and simply stirs up memories in the horse's mind of the wrong way to do things.

With a right-handed horse it is always the right rein that is raised, even when circling to the left, because whichever way it is turning, the horse is still right-handed! Do not raise both hands, because this creates a false bend or "break" at the base of the neck just in front of the withers. Of course, your hand must be lowered again afterward. *The straighter the horse is, the less the rider needs to do.* Once the horse stops leaning on its right shoulder, return your hand to its normal position.

Riding a right-handed horse on the left rein

We know that when a right-handed horse is ridden on the *left rein* it becomes *concave* to the left, that centrifugal forces cause the right shoulder to fall out, and that the hindquarters follow suit. In this situation, you need to sit square to the horse, with a light pressure on the inside stirrup. Work more with an outside flexion, starting at the beginning of the circle next to the fence, so to be ready for the part of the circle across the center of the arena, which is where the "falling out" is most noticeable.

The reason the outside flexion should be practiced first on the sections of the circle that are next to the fence, as in the photo below, is because the fence or a wall prevents the horse being thrown outward by centrifugal force. Once the horse can easily be flexed to the outside, the counter-flexion can be performed on the unsupported side of the circle, away from the fence. Repeat this exercise four or five times, then resume the normal, inside flexion.

Note

It is important that after asking for, and obtaining the outside flexion, you bring your right hand up toward you. Do not do so before you have brought your right shoulder back. By changing between inside and outside flexion in movement, you are swapping the support and free leg, and teaching the horse to stay flexible in its hips. This also results in the horse developing more impulsion, and a more "uphill" way of going.

Here, Doris is riding another right-handed horse on the left rein. She is riding with an outside flexion to counteract centrifugal force.

Everything the horse has learned on the longe during its straightness training must be translated into work under saddle. So you need to instill a new understanding of the aids.

In our experience, the way the aids are usually taught makes it difficult for the horse to understand them. We are convinced that in many cases, the horse has never grasped their meaning and is confused by them. It is strange that a rider is taught the aids in stages, but the horse is taught them almost as a "package." It is not surprising that misunderstandings arise. The strength with which seat, leg and rein aids have been used from the outset is part of the problem with many of the horses that come to the Center for retraining. Leg aids can do the most damage, because they are often too hard, for example, when the horse tries to resist because too much has been asked of it. The rider tries to "ride the horse through it" with his legs. And, why does a rider use his legs more strongly at this point? *Usually because everything else has failed!*

Seat and leg aids

We have already discussed the rein aids and the part they play in the horse's retraining. Let us now turn our attention to the seat and leg aids. What is the secret behind these aids? Horse and rider have similarities. Both have a longitudinal axis, and so a "balancing pole." In one, the longitudinal axis is vertical, whilst in the other, it is horizontal. In both cases, the longitudinal axis is involved in balance. In man, it is used to enable him to balance in an upright position. The horse, on the other hand, needs it to support itself in a horizontal position, because the forehand and trunk are constantly "running away" from the hindquarters. This is the big difference. So when horse and rider are "directly connected," that is, when the vertical (the rider's vertical axis) is aligned with the horizontal (the horse's horizontal axis), the rider, through his behavior, can exercise considerable influence over the horse. This influence is dependent on the rider's seat and the way he uses it. *This is why, of all the aids, the seat aids are the most important.*

You must do things in a slow, progressive manner to avoid overtaxing the horse and maybe causing resistance. So, in the ridden training that follows the longe work, do not use your legs, at first. This is important, because many horses—through too strong use of leg aids—have tended to "run away from the leg," that is, they rush forward and lose their balance. Usually they fall onto the shoulders, further increasing the heaviness on the forehand.

If the legs are used too soon after the straightness training longe work, the horse reacts just the same as it did before the corrective training, or it fails to respond to the leg at all. You must therefore create this intermediate stage as a "bridge" in the training.

Interval training to increase activity of the hindquarters

Once you have understood this important point, you'll realize that you must then extend the influence of your seat to the hindquarters. You do this through what we call interval training. It is another big test of the rider's "feel" and patience.

A horse that has only been taught to respond to the leg aids now needs to learn to respond to the seat. By tightening your back muscles, you should be able to send your horse forward—in walk, trot and even extended trot—without using your legs. It works! Have patience! Once again, you use the horse's shoulder as the starting point: on a right-handed horse, touch the *right shoulder* with the whip at the same time as you tighten your back muscles. On no account must the whip be used on the hindquarters. Never forget that shear and centrifugal forces are at work behind you! Only when these forces have been brought under control should you start to use the whip on the hindquarters again.

After the horse has moved forward in response to these aids (back and whip), halt and do the same thing again. The whip should be used with great care. It should only be applied if the horse has not understood your seat aids. Once the horse will walk forward from the halt, the next stage is the trot.

Remember, you are doing this work in preparation for the use of your legs, which will come later. The purpose of this stage in the training is to gain control of the horse's center of gravity. The aim is to be able to ride forward without the risk of the horse falling onto its forehand. Using your seat, push the horse on in trot, then bring it back again as soon as you feel it starting to fall onto its shoulders. How do you do this? Tighten your back muscles and lift the horse's right shoulder. The rein aids for this exercise were described earlier on p. 97. The combination of rein and seat aids is crucial. This exercise should be performed repeatedly until you can feel the horse starting to step under itself with its hind feet.

The seat should always be used a split second before the legs.

It is important that the horse can be pushed on in trot by use of the seat alone. It is even more important for training that the horse can then be "brought back" simply by relaxing the back muscles a little, and at the same time acting on the right shoulder. You will notice that your back muscles need to be tightened less and less each time to get the horse to step under. The intensity of the aids should gradually be "stepped down" until the horse responds to the lightest of pressure. Then, and only then, can you cautiously begin to use your legs. You will then experience what you have been trying to achieve for a long time: the horse will go forward with energy and spring, and without rushing. At the same time, you will learn to act with your seat a split second before your legs. This teaches the horse to respond first to the seat aids—by stepping under and becoming more "uphill."

We need to discuss the leg aids in detail, because they are another of the tools we use to correct the horse's crookedness.

Interaction between the rider's shoulder and leg

Let us begin by looking back at the effects of crookedness as described in the previous chapters. (Remember, we are discussing a right-handed horse.) The first things that come to mind are shear and centrifugal forces.

The *shear* force occurs on the right rein owing to the horse using its right shoulder to brace itself and the hindquarters swing out.

The "usual" way to prevent this is by vigorous use of the outside (left) leg. If you've paid careful attention to what we have said so far, you will see that this does not make sense.

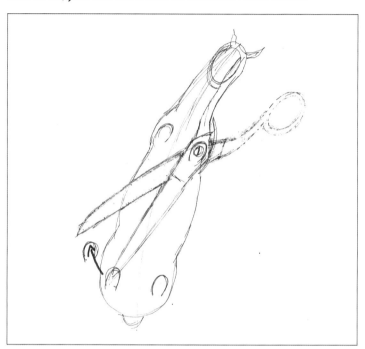

The action of shear forces (see also p. 44).

This is because the cause of the hindquarters swinging outward is the diagonally opposite shoulder, so you will not be able to solve the problem by using your outside leg. On the contrary, since the horse is not yet established in its new way of going, using the outside leg this way simply causes the weight to be thrown back onto the right shoulder again.

In other words, all your good work in moving the horse's center of gravity back diagonally toward the outside hind leg is wasted by premature use of your outside leg.

Let us look at what you've done so far. You have used the right rein to move the weight back toward the outside hind leg and lift the right shoulder. If you continue patiently along this road, you'll manage to get the horse to lift its right shoulder sufficiently to bring the left side of its rib cage outward to meet your left leg.

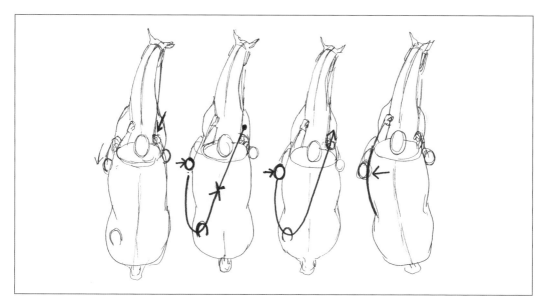

The rib cage becomes convex (instead of the usual concave with shear force) on this side, allowing your outside leg to be used correctly *in a regulating or guarding capacity*, that is, passively, *without pushing the quarters in*. (Later, however, this will also make it easier for the horse to understand the sideways-pushing action of this outside leg.) The horse is now not only straight to the track, but is also working at a higher level, with rhythm and impulsion, and swinging through its back.

Bringing the right shoulder up and back so that the horse's rib cage "comes out to meet" the rider's outside leg. Note the position and action of the right rein. See also the photo on p. 98.

Flexion and bend

Riding is impossible without flexion. This cannot be over-stressed. Yet, how often do we see a rider going along the long side of the school with his horse's head straight? When questioned, he replies "But on straight lines you ride without flexion." This is an incorrect, even "dangerous" assumption.

To understand this you need to go back to the beginning of this book, and reflect on the part played by the *longissimus* muscle in transferring the weight onto the forelegs (for example when the horse kicks), and thus making the horse heavy in front (p. 23). As you already know, this condition is inseparable from crookedness, so there is most of the explanation. All that remains is to remember the straightness training longe work, and how we "ask" the horse to yield in its neck and flex to enable us to influence the shoulder on the side in question (see p. 79). As has been explained, we then "translate" this into work under saddle, and continue to influence the horse in this way until the balance is established.

And what about bend? Should bend and flexion be considered together? What is flexion, and what effect does it have on the horse's body? Let us try to explain it without a diagram. Stand with your legs slightly apart and drop your right shoulder. Do not push it down, simply let it go.

You can now feel that the whole of your right side, down to your hip, has relaxed and softened. This is "flexion," and it affects the whole body as far as the hip. Now, while still in this position, bend your upper body, above the hips, to the right. This is "bend."

Now, stiffen your neck and shoulders and try to bend your body again. It doesn't work! So we can deduce from this that flexion is a necessary precondition for bend. If you translate this from the vertical to the horizontal, you will see how it applies to the horse.

We can also deduce from this that bend is the next "stage" on from flexion. Hence it follows that, especially on the horse's right side, if flexion does not give us the necessary control over the shoulder, then we need to use bend.

So, after flexion comes bend. Since controlling the shoulders increases your ability to influence the hindquarters, it follows that flexion and bend are very important, and an absolute necessity in the transition from longe work to ridden work. They enable you to control the position of the horse's center of gravity, and also the diagonal movement of its weight. Once you get the horse to yield, you are on the way to getting it to move freely and through its back.

In our opinion, too much importance is attached to crooked-ness in the rider. We must not forget that professional trainers are human, and thus crooked in their bodies, but despite this, they can sort out a horse's problem once they understand it. If they can manage, why shouldn't "normal" riders be able to do so? It is simply a question of approach. Very often, riders are made to rely too much on their trainers instead of being encouraged to be independent: they fail to develop their "feel" for balance, so they are constantly "chasing after" the center of gravity. The horse falls out through its shoulder, and takes the rider with it. The rider then attempts to regain control by pull-ing. The rider's weight unbalances the horse even further, and a vicious circle develops. An experienced trainer looks at things differently. In this situation, to keep control he would correct the horse's balance, for example, by changing from an inside to an outside flexion. It is part of our task, during the transition from the straightness training longe work to ridden work, to develop the independence and self-confidence of the rider. We are con-vinced that if this were standard practice there would be more sound horses—and this would be only one of many benefits.

Keeping the horse correctly aligned with the circle
For the reasons we have explained, the horse's shoulders are, in our opinion, the rider's most important source of information. They tell you about the hindquarters.

Understanding this may make it a bit easier to understand the established principles of training, and indeed, even shed new light on them. However, if you are not making any head-way by following the "rules" it is perfectly acceptable to look for an alternative way of doing things (and it may turn out that this alternative is not as new as it seems!) When the horse is bent and on a curved track, if you find it difficult to keep the hind-quarters following in the tracks of the forehand (particularly

A right-handed horse on a right bend leaning on, or propping itself up with its inside forefoot.

in the case of a right-handed horse on the right rein), the next logical step must be to look beyond the "rule book," and ask yourself why.

Riding a right-handed horse on a circle to the right is a good way to get it to demonstrate how its crookedness affects it on this rein. As you circle away from the fence or wall, you'll notice that the horse stays on the circle of its own accord. It leans into the circle and "lands heavily" on its right foot. Even if you try to argue that the horse has stayed on the circle in response to your aids, this does not alter the fact that it is leaning inward. This means that it is relying more on the right *foreleg* than the inside *hind leg* for support. You can feel it from the saddle. Further away from the wall, the horse loses impulsion, and you can also feel the hindquarters drifting outward slightly. So does this mean you should use more outside leg and ride the horse forward more? Remember what we said on p. 104 about shear forces and the use of the outside leg!

Try to use the horse's shoulder to solve the problem. Before you leave the wall, lift the horse's right shoulder as described earlier on pp. 77 to 101—helped, of course, by the positioning of your own center of gravity—until you can clearly feel the outward curve of the horse's rib cage under your outside leg. You almost have to ride shoulder-in, until eventually the horse starts to step with its inside hind foot under its center of gravity. Then, you can finally bend the horse to the circle. Of course, the circle is not perfect at first: it is egg-shaped. However, the horse is working with much more impulsion. Your main aim to begin with is to maintain and establish this impulsion. To do this you must avoid "pressurizing" the horse, which leads instead to loss of impulsion and a tense, hurried way of going. Then, start working gradually toward obtaining a correct circle. One of the principle requirements for this is that the horse's body remains correctly aligned with the circle; that it is not crooked. After a while, it becomes second nature to the horse to follow with its hindquarters along the same track as its forehand. For all this work you need to have a "feel" for the horse's balance. This is learned by practice.

You cannot find what you cannot feel.

Adjusting the position of the horse's center of gravity

We refer here to repeated changes of flexion away from, and back toward the shoulder that the horse is leaning on, that is, the right shoulder in a right-handed horse. The horse needs to be fully familiar with the aids for flexing away from and toward the shoulder. Specifically, these aids are both reins as well as your body, especially the inside knee and the outside leg's contact on the horse's convex rib cage.

Let us begin—again with a right-handed horse—on the right rein. You need to remember that on this rein the horse tends to throw its weight onto its inside foreleg, which causes shear forces to develop. You know what problems these forces cause, so they need to be targeted through special training.

What is happening in the drawing below is that the horse is being flexed to the left, which prompts a movement of the center of gravity toward the right shoulder. This is something that happens naturally in any four-legged animal. Since it is

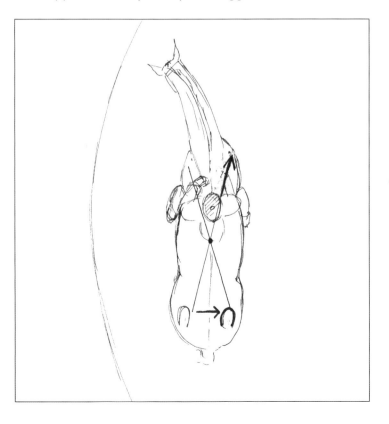

⬤ When the horse is flexed to the outside on a circle to the right, the horse's center of gravity drifts toward the right, and the movement of the right hind (the "free leg") is blocked. This is a natural response and the rider should use it to straighten the horse in his corrective training. See drawing on p. 110.

in accordance with natural laws, you should make use of it in your corrective training to straighten the horse. At the same time, the horse changes its "support" and "free" leg. Remember that the problem of crookedness has not been resolved until the horse can switch its support and free leg without problem when you change the rein.

Immediately changing from counter (outside) flexion to normal (inside) flexion changes the picture (see the drawings below and on p. 111).

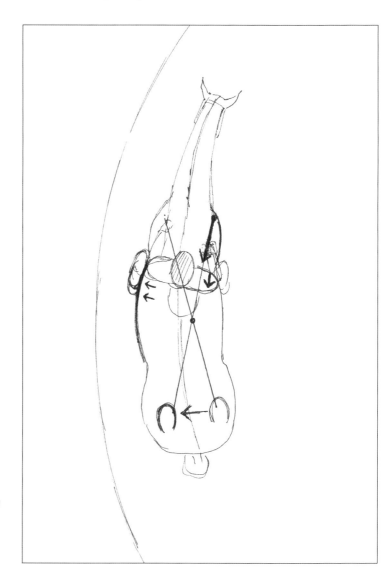

To continue from the drawing on p. 109, when changing from outside to inside flexion, the horse brings its right shoulder back. Its center of gravity moves backward toward the center of the horse's body. The horse changes its support and "free leg."

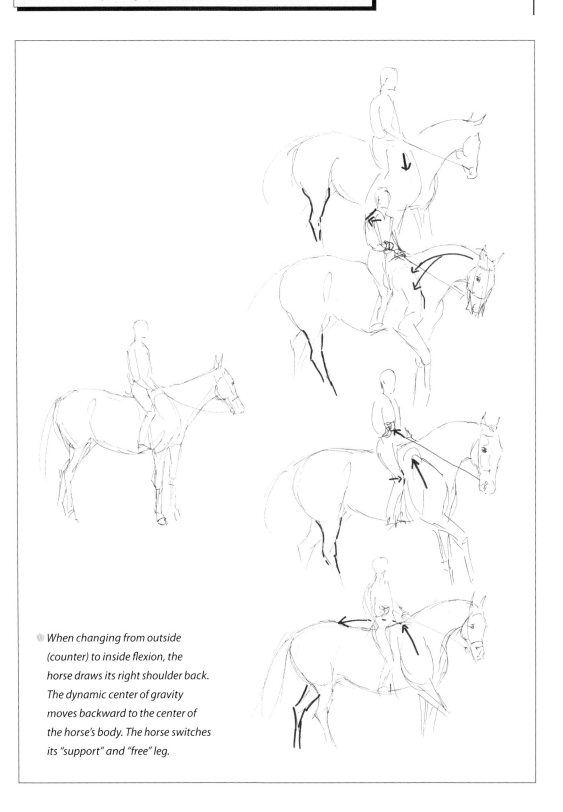

When changing from outside (counter) to inside flexion, the horse draws its right shoulder back. The dynamic center of gravity moves backward to the center of the horse's body. The horse switches its "support" and "free" leg.

When flexion is changed from the outside to the inside (see drawings on pp. 109 to 111), the horse lifts its right shoulder (note arrow) and switches its support leg and free leg. The rider's right shoulder comes back, his right knee presses from right to left, and the horse's left side becomes convex so that the rib cage "comes out to meet" the rider's left leg.

The center of gravity, which was tending to move toward the right shoulder, moves back toward the center of the horse's body, and it is the left hind leg that becomes the support leg. After frequent repetition of this exercise, the rider will clearly feel an increase in the impulsion and activity of the hindquarters, and a lifting of the horse's back underneath him.

What should you do at this point? Since this is what we call "interval training", once the horse has obtained the inside flexion, you should yield both reins and ride the horse forward. The horse learns from this to move off and step forward smartly and, what is very important, it begins to take much more ground-covering strides.

As shown in the drawings on p. 111, the aids for moving the center of gravity backward from the shoulder toward the opposite hind leg are as already described above: inside flexion, then lift the horse's shoulder, weight on the inside seat bone to relieve the left side and allow the center of gravity to move backward toward your left leg. It is important for you to bring your right shoulder back. The horse's left side becomes convex—the rib cage "comes out to meet your left leg." Your right knee is now very important. At the point when the horse's shoulder is lifted, the pressure from the knee plays a supporting role in the backward movement of the horse's center of gravity. Think here of your leg as acting on the hindquarters, and your knee acting on the shoulders. What do the reins do? The outside rein, which has "obtained" the outside flexion, remains in the same position, whilst the inside rein asks for the new, inside flexion. The horse then yields and softens through its body. All this is good preparation for getting the horse to take a correct contact on the outside rein: you are gradually getting the horse used to the outside rein and outside leg.

The next stage is to ride on the left rein (see drawing on this page). The horse's neck now has a pronounced bend to the

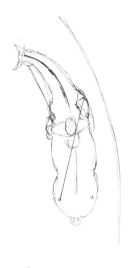

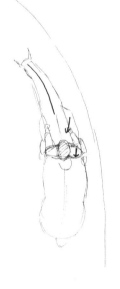

From exaggerated neck bend back to normal left flexion (see also drawing on p. 113).

inside, so that the right side and shoulder are convex. Centrifugal force throws the horse—or, as we might say, it's center of gravity—outward through its convex outside shoulder. By raising the outside rein (do not lift the hand above chest height) you correct this exaggerated bend of the neck to the left, and transform it into left flexion. However, it is important not to turn this into an outside (right) flexion.

As a result of this exercise and correct flexion, the upward rounding of the horse's back becomes even more pronounced, so the horse works with even greater freedom and impulsion (see drawings above).

Note that when you bring the (right) rein toward your chest, your right shoulder should be drawn back, and the line from the horse's mouth, through the rein and hand to your shoulder, should run almost parallel to the side of the horse's neck and shoulder. This allows you to lift the horse's shoulder rather than its head. To apply the aids, little more has to be done, except that when the bend is changed into flexion, your outside shoulder should be drawn back slightly to reduce the weight on the horse's outside shoulder.

The rule is that at this stage in training, with a right-handed horse, it is always the right rein that is responsible for the flexion. When working in a clockwise direction (to the right) its action is *direct* and when working counterclockwise, it becomes the outside rein, and its action is *indirect*. It is best to do all these exercises on a circle. The biggest problem with these exercises is usually in the rider's mind. It is not that he cannot understand, but he keeps thinking that this is no use at all for riding in competition. Unfortunately, working with freedom and looseness is not widely practiced. If you are training only with the next competition in mind, you will end up riding "mechanically." This results in loss of "feel" and the development of tension. It is the horse that suffers.

THE BIT

How does the bit work?

The purpose of the bit is to provide the rider with the means to receive information from the horse, and transmit information to it. This information forms the basis for communication between rider and horse. Communication is a way of reaching an agreement or understanding, and so is a two-way process. As we have said, to communicate, we need to use the language that is most easily understood by the horse, which is body language and, in this case, the bit.

We should begin by discussing what sort of bit we recommend: a *simple snaffle* or a *double-jointed snaffle*? In our opinion, the best bit for basic training is the simple snaffle. This is because flexion is an essential part of basic training, and we obtain flexion only through the use of a simple, single-jointed snaffle. Use of a bit with a solid, unbroken mouthpiece is reserved for horses and riders who are established in their basic training. So how does a simple, single-jointed snaffle work? As can be seen from the description of the training, the influence of the bit needs to extend as far as the horse's hip.

To recap: the *longissimus* muscle runs from the atlas (the head) to the sacrum (the croup). Flexion entails the yielding of this muscle on one side. At this point, we need to look at the action of the double-jointed snaffle and compare it to the single-jointed snaffle. The action of these two bits on the shoulders is very different, and as should be clear by now, control of the shoulders is of paramount importance. We feel that, if used for the purposes of our corrective straightness training as described so far, a double-jointed bit can cause problems. Its negative influence can be seen most clearly when we try to lift the horse's right shoulder (in a right-handed horse): the middle section of the mouthpiece rubs against the corner of the mouth and the cheek, provoking resistance. This is counterproductive, and so not recommended, because it makes both "feel" and accuracy impossible. For this work, a single-jointed bit gives us better control over the hindquarters, and therefore gives a better result.

However, we might also ask whether the mildness, or otherwise, of the bit is the main consideration. In the light of what we have written on the subject of flexion, it could be argued that skill and understanding are more important than the "strength" of the bit.

Next, we need to examine the action of the double-jointed bit, and look at how it produces flexion. When, through the reins, we ask for a flexion to the right or left, any bit comes out of the right or left side of the mouth slightly. This is unavoidable. With a simple, single-jointed snaffle, this does not cause a problem. However, in the case of a double-jointed snaffle, the first joint rubs on the side of the mouth as it does when we lift the horse's shoulder. Horses often respond to this by resisting. The neck is involved in this, which means that flexion is affected. The rider then tends to react by using his hand more strongly than he should.

These observations on bits and their use are not meant as criticism; we are simply looking for explanations, and trying to help you identify the reasons why your horse may not be going as you would like it to.

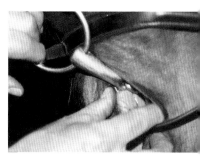

What happens to a double-jointed bit when the rider asks for flexion? Top: This photo shows the bit in the mouth before flexion is requested. Bottom: By simulating pressure on the ring and opening the horse's mouth to show the tongue, the person is clearly showing that the outside link of the bit rubs backward and forward on the corner of the mouth.

5

Working with
Other Professionals

Crookedness and its effects

If we look at the evolutionary history of the horse, it quickly becomes clear that horses are not designed to live in barns or stables. In the wild they walk for long distances every day with their heads down, grazing. We do not allow for this, and instead horses are usually kept inside. This is done because of outside space restrictions, and also because grazing is hard to come by. And when we keep horses out together in small fields, disputes arise over the pecking order, which cause difficulty. Also, competition horses cannot achieve peak performance if they are left out 24 hours a day. All these problems associated with keeping horses at grass are well known, but this does not alter the fact that today's horse is still a creature of wide open spaces. If you want to keep your horse sound and healthy, and enable it to achieve its potential, you need to take its living conditions into account and ensure a suitable system of management. Also, the exercise or work regime must be suited to the way the horse is kept.

Through attention to breeding, the quality of horses bred in Germany has improved more and more in recent years. It is now unusual to find serious conformation defects in German riding horses. Thanks to improved diagnostic techniques in veterinary medicine, it has become easier to identify defects, and these are then taken into account by breeders. Yet, in spite of all the work that has been done, more and more horses are becoming lame for no apparent reason. X-rays may reveal minor irregularities, but usually veterinary treatment has little effect. In these cases, what is the connection between the horse's work and its health and soundness?

Movement and balance

To train the horse, you need to understand how it moves and be able to apply this knowledge to its practical work. As a basis for every form of ridden work, the horse needs to be taught to carry the rider. You also need to be able to ensure that, once learned, this ability is not lost.

Without help, the horse cannot carry the rider without coming to harm. Like everyone who practices sport, it needs appro-

TINA RASCH, VETERINARY PRACTITIONER

priate training. No sportsman would take part in a competition without the necessary preparation, and the same applies to a horse. The horse must be given specific training to prepare its body. Its muscles and metabolism must be able to cope with all the demands made on them by its work. The horse is dependent on its rider for this preparation. Only when you have an understanding of the way the horse moves can you train it meaningfully. If you fail to notice the signs of tension caused by muscle stiffness, pushing the horse too hard, an ill-fitting saddle, problems with the teeth, incorrect shoeing or foot care, or wrong feeding, or simply fail to recognize that the horse is having a bad day, then things will go wrong. No one, man or horse, can learn whilst under permanent pressure. They "turn off" and lose interest. Pain is reflected in the horse's action. It shows signs of lameness, or takes a shorter step with one leg than the other. The (often lengthy) search for the cause then begins.

The horse's anatomy

The horse is a creature of flight. It is "front-heavy" and is affected by a natural innate crookedness. Its heaviness on the forehand is anatomically based. As in all objects with moving parts, the position of the center of gravity in the horse does not remain constant. Two examples, when the horse has a very full belly or when it raises its head, the center of gravity moves backward.

As soon as the horse lowers its head and neck (or when its belly is empty), its center of gravity moves forward.

A stationary horse more easily loses its balance forward or sideways than backward, because its center of gravity is closer to its front and lateral supports (its front feet) than to its rear ones.

What are the consequences of carrying a rider?

The weight of the rider causes the horse's center of gravity to move even further forward. There are two things the horse can do to compensate:

1. It can raise its head and neck.
2. It can try to find its balance by moving forward.

A horse that rushes forward with its head in the air is not necessarily being disobedient; it is probably just trying to find its balance. If we use auxiliary reins, such as draw reins to force the horse into a position, the horse may look better, but we have made no progress at all in solving the problem.

As soon you take the draw reins off, the head goes up and the horse charges forward again. The heaviness in front remains a problem until you recognize it and do something about it.

The whole of the horse's body is designed for forward movement. The center of gravity is nearer to the front of the base of support, and moves even further forward when the horse puts its head down. The forward movement is initiated by extending the hind legs and pushing off with the hind feet. Provided the surface is firm, when these joints open and the limb extended, the pressure exerted on the ground is converted into forward thrust. The pelvis determines the direction of movement and transmits this to the body.

The body

Think of the horse's body as built like a suspension bridge. (See earlier discussion and illustration on p. 26). In the horse, the abdominal muscles correspond to the "road," and they are "suspended" from the "arch" framework: the arch consists of the entire thoracic and lumbar section of the spine, the pelvis and pelvic muscles, and the ligaments. The elasticity is provided by the intervertebral discs, the ligaments between the spinous processes (*ligamenta interspinale*), and between adjacent vertebrae (*ligamenta flava*), the neck ligament and long back ligament, and in particular by the muscle tone of the long and short back muscles. The two ends of the arch are connected through the breast bone, the *linea alba* and the abdominal muscles. The bodies of the vertebrae and the intervertebral discs provide resistance to downward pressure, while the resistance to upward pressure is provided by the spine (the vertebral bodies and the joints connecting them), the spinous processes, their interconnecting ligaments, and the tendons of the *musculi spinales* and the *musculus longissimus*. The spinous processes have no static function, but serve as "lever arms" for the muscles.

The advantage of this form of construction is that the forces to which the back is subjected (pressure, stretch and pull) are not transmitted to the limbs. This means that if the horse is working with an upwardly curved back, taut abdominal muscles and an arched neck, the strain is taken by the "bridge," so the legs are spared.

The problem is that instead of moving like this, many riding horses go with their backs hollow and their heads in the air.

The consequences

The arch of the bridge is protected from sagging, on the one hand, by the taut "roadway" (that is, by the abdominal muscles) and by active contraction of the muscles, and on the other, by the mechanical limitation on the movement caused by the articular processes wedging against each other, and the tips of the spinous processes drawing together until they meet.

In the wild, a healthy horse's back is hollowed only when the horse brings its head up, for example to scent the air, or when running away with its head high. Otherwise, the horse spends most of its time grazing, with its head down, or walking around with its head and neck only partially raised. In these positions, the spinous processes of the thoracic vertebrae move apart, and the thoracic spine bends.

In riding horses, on the other hand, when the horse is ridden with its head in the air, it will inevitably go with its back hollow, and so with the tips of the spinous processes close together. This is how, over time, "kissing spines" develops.

So, the rider has a two-fold task ahead of him. First, he needs to balance his horse, so that it stops trying to balance itself by putting its head up, then he needs to get it to work with its back curved upward. To do this, the horse needs to use its abdominal muscles.

In the horse (as in man), the muscles along the top of the back and neck, and on the back of the thigh, work hand in hand with those of the underside of the neck, the abdominal region and the front of the thigh. If you bend forward from a standing position, you contract the muscles on the front of your neck, in your abdomen and on the front of your thigh. To return to an upright position, you lift your head, and contract your back muscles. The same thing happens with the horse, the only difference being that it is standing on all fours. The same principle applies: the horse rounds its back and contracts its abdominal muscles when it lowers its head. If, in movement, the horse contracts its abdominal muscles, curves its head downward, and so lifts its back, it will have no problem lowering its hindquarters, and it will go more "uphill."

The success of the training is easiest to judge in trot. This is because the legs work in diagonal pairs, so the two legs of the pair move almost in unison for the whole sequence of the movement.

If the horse is in balance, when it is ridden in trot, the right foreleg will swing forward parallel to the left hind leg. In contrast, if the horse is ridden with its head and neck raised and its back hollow, the steps will be tense, and the hind leg will no longer swing forward parallel to the foreleg.

The movement of the hind leg is then upward instead of forward, and impulsion is lost. The hind leg can no longer step forward under the center of gravity, and so cannot work in conjunction with the abdominal muscles to lift the back. The horse is forced to contract the muscles along the top of its back in order to move forward. When these muscles contract, they shorten, drawing the tips of the spinous processes closer together. Also, when the muscles in the top of the back are tightened, those along the top of the neck contract at the same time, and the horse throws its head up.

A horse that is worked in this way over a long period develops muscle pain in its back, loses muscle from its hindquarters, and the underside of the neck becomes overdeveloped. Because of the tightened back muscles, the spinous processes of the thoracic and lumbar vertebrae rub against each other, and "kissing spines" develops. If the abdominal muscles are slack and the back is sagging, spring and elasticity are lost, and the full force of the movement has to be absorbed by the joints of the legs and feet. This increases the risk of arthritis.

In addition to this, the joints are also subjected to the effects of the horse's innate crookedness.

As has been explained earlier, like people, horses are either right-handed or left-handed. Very few of them are equally well coordinated on both sides. As well as the problems for the rider, this can lead to health and soundness problems.

Because of this crookedness, the horse's body has to contend with two kinds of force: centrifugal and shear force.

Centrifugal forces act on the *forehand,* when the horse is in movement. As a result of centrifugal forces when working on a curved or circular track, the horse's body is carried outward and the speed of the movement increases. The bigger the circle and the faster the movement, the greater the centrifugal force. To counteract this force, and to prevent falling, the horse braces itself with its strongest foreleg. In the case of a right-handed horse, this is the right foreleg. When the weight is anchored on this right foreleg while the horse is moving, the rest of the horse's body rotates around it, especially when turning to the right.

The consequences of shear force, on the other hand, are more likely to affect the hindquarters. (For complete discussion of centrifugal and shear forces, see p. 39.)

AILMENTS THAT RESULT FROM CROOKEDNESS

Example 1: Navicular Disease

Navicular disease affects the navicular bone, the end of the deep flexor tendon, which attaches to it, and the synovial bursa (joint oil capsule) that lies between the navicular bone and the flexor tendon. Diagnosis is usually by clinical examination, X-rays, and possibly, nerve-blocking. In most of the horses affected, the findings are the same in both front feet, but the horse is lame on one side only, namely, in a right-handed horse, on the right side.

A right-handed horse relies more and more on its right leg. This means that in movement it puts a greater proportion of the weight on its right front foot. If the horse is heavy in front as well as crooked, the problem is even greater.

Because the back is "swinging" downward, the joints of the forelimbs take the full force of the movement. In a right-handed horse, there is more strain on the right leg than the left, so the right navicular bone is affected before the left. Since the horse is working on a curved or circular track, the navicular bone is also affected by centrifugal forces, which cause further trauma to it.

Example 2: Sacroiliac Joint Problems

Right-handed horses that are also heavy in front frequently display signs of pain in the sacroiliac region. If you watch such a horse being longed on a left-hand circle, you will notice that it falls out through its right shoulder. It speeds up, because its center of gravity has crossed to the outside of the pivot point, and the rest of the body is "chasing" the shoulders as they fall outward.

The horse starts to "go wide" behind, placing strain on the sacroiliac joint.

Example 3: Patellar Ligament Strain

A right-handed horse being longed to the right turns its body outward around its right forefoot. In anticipation of the weight landing on its left hind foot, the horse turns its left hind leg outward, and puts the foot down pointing outward. The shear forces push the rest of the body outward over this foot, and to keep its balance the horse is then forced to turn its left hind leg inward.

These examples show clearly that soundness problems can be the result of training. If problems are not identified promptly, symptoms of lameness and unsoundness will arise, and a long-term problem develops. Often the "unlevelness" is so ingrained that the horse still presents as lame even under the influence of painkillers or a nerve block.

This problem is recognized in human medicine. Like people, horses need physiotherapy or special training in order to change the way they move. Without this help, they become progressively stiffer and unsteadier in their way of going, which is very stressful for any creature of flight. By working to counteract this heaviness in front and crookedness, you can prevent injury to the horse and also improve existing problems and make the horse sound again.

However much attention is paid to soundness when breeding, if you do not take the anatomical considerations into

Tina Rasch
Praktische Tierärztin
(Veterinary Practitioner)
Alter Weseler Strasse 41
D-47475 Kamp Lintfort
Germany

account when you ride a horse, damage to the locomotive system is inevitable.

DR. MED. VET. MARTINA STEINMETZ

Acupuncture, holistic treatments and the integrated approach to tackling crookedness

The horse's inborn crookedness—and its significance when training—was recognized centuries ago by trainers. However, little attention is paid to it today in veterinary medicine, despite the fact that it has a decisive influence on the way the horse moves and on its long-term usability as a riding horse. The principle behind any method of training is systematic gymnastic schooling aimed at developing the horse's physical and mental capabilities. Correcting crookedness and making the horse straight are the hardest part. Only when both sides of the body are equally developed in terms of strength and agility can the horse's weight be distributed equally on both sides, and premature wear avoided. If crookedness is not corrected, health and soundness problems will be the outcome.

Causes and manifestations of laterality and inborn crookedness

Nowadays, natural crookedness is usually attributed to *laterality* (favoring one side over the other). Laterality is the general term used to describe morphological (physical), functional and sensory manifestations of symmetry or asymmetry between paired organs.

Included in this concept are hemispherical dominance and limb dominance, or "handedness" (that is, right- or left-handedness). Various studies on the subject have concluded that the asymmetries that manifest themselves as the favoring of one side affect the ability to learn movements and to cope in stress situations.

However, following trauma, injury, or any event that results in loss of function (of the brain or limbs, for example), the laterality can change, because new ways to do things must, and can be learned. Through specific training, one-sidedness can be improved.

When a foal is suckling or beginning to eat grass, it is noticeable that it stands with its legs apart, and usually with the same foreleg advanced. As it grows older, it continues to adopt this position. In its stall or box also, it stands with its favorite foot forward to eat its hay off the floor. Turns are usually made in the same direction: when standing at ease in a stall or box (which, for the average horse accounts for 60 percent of the day) the weight is transferred backward and forward from one foot to the other as many as a hundred times per hour, with one leg favored over the other as the support leg. By so doing, the horse further reinforces its laterality and crookedness.

We must remember that horses are designed to move—straight ahead—for more than 16 hours per day to select suitable food to eat.

Asymmetries and their effects on the horse's way of going have been identified and discussed in many motion studies. It has also been shown that the "kinematic fingerprint," that is, each horse's personal, unique pace or characteristic pattern of movement, does not alter when the horse is ridden, but instead becomes much more pronounced. For example, most young horses prefer left canter, jump with their left leg leading, and in walk and trot take steps of a different length with one diagonal pair of legs than with the other, and this behavior becomes even more noticeable when the horse is first ridden.

Very well-trained jumping horses lead with their inside leg—the leg corresponding to the curve of the track. Racehorses go round bends with the inside leg leading, and change legs on the straight to prevent overworking one side. With a good dressage horse, you see a higher-than-normal degree of symmetry in the length of the steps.

Effects on the way of going and the locomotive system

A crooked horse can be described more or less as follows (see drawings on p. 129):

In walk and trot especially, the forehand and hindquarters are out of alignment. One diagonal pair of legs steps further forward and under, while the other diagonal pair *pushes* more than it steps under. In the halt, the horse does not stand square, but stands with one diagonal pair of legs in front of the other (similar to the way it stood for grazing, as discussed earlier). One diagonal pair of legs is ahead of its ideal position, and the other behind it. The first diagonal pair is described as the *supporting diagonal,* the second as the *pushing* (or thrust-developing) *diagonal.* Usually, the horse is crooked in that the hind foot of the pushing diagonal is carried inward and set down near the horse's longitudinal axis, and the hind leg of the "supporting diagonal" steps and is set down to the side of the horse's body.

The loading on the horse's locomotive system is asymmetrical because of, and in proportion to the crookedness of the gait.

● The forefoot of the *pushing diagonal* pair steps, and is set down behind its ideal position. Too much weight is placed on the toe, and too little on the heel. The hind foot of this diagonal also moves and is set down behind its ideal position and deviates inward, so that too much weight is placed on the toe and outer wall of the foot. On this diagonal, it is the muscles that extend the joints—the extensor muscles—that do most of the work.

● The forefoot of the *supporting diagonal* pair moves and is set down in front of its ideal position, with too much of the weight on the heel. The diagonally opposite hind foot also moves and is set down in front of its ideal position, and deviates outward slightly. Hence, too much weight is placed on the heels and inner wall of the foot. On this diagonal, it is the muscles that are used to carry the body and flex the joints—the *flexor muscles*—that do most of the work.

The more pronounced the crookedness, the greater the imbalance between the workload of the flexors and extensors, and so the more pronounced the imbalance of the hoof.

Normally, a muscle adapts to an increase in workload by increasing in size, meaning mass. However, if it is forced to work while tense, which it is not designed to do for any length of time, it will decrease in volume, causing atrophy. If the extensor and flexor muscles of a joint do not work harmoniously together, the joint will not be either fully flexed or fully extended, depending on whether it is the flexor or extensor muscles that have the "upper hand." The movement of the joint is "blocked" by the muscles.

The hoof also responds to the increased weight, and so

increased wear, by increasing the growth of horn in the affected areas. When excessive weight is brought to bear on one part
of the foot, wear and growth are no longer in balance, the part
of the wall affected becomes more upright and shorter, and the
heels become shallow and contracted. Furthermore, each foreleg and each hind leg develops in the opposite way to the one
next to it, making the problem worse: in one forefoot the wall
is more upright, and in the other forefoot, it is shallow and the
heels contracted (seen from the back, the bottom of the foot is
narrower than the top). Since the spine at the withers is "slung"
between the two forelegs, this uneven development is enough
to cause tension and restriction (muscle blocks) in this area.

The suspensory ligament of the upright forefoot is under a lot
of stress, both because the foot is more upright and because it
is set down behind its ideal position. In the shallow foot, there is
enormous strain on the flexor muscles. Since the tendon of one
of these flexor muscles, the deep flexor tendon, passes over the
navicular bone, if the heels are also contracted, this will predis-
pose the horse to navicular problems.

The hind legs are similarly affected, but here the situation is
made worse by the twisting effect on the legs and feet. Here too,
joint, ligament and muscle problems can be the consequence.

As the bridge between the fore- and hind limbs, the back
plays an important part in the movement. Here, since it has to
counteract and compensate for the uneven steps, the rhythm
is affected, and the horse cannot swing through its back.

Acupuncture

Acupuncture is a method of treatment based on maintaining
balance, namely the balance between Yin and Yang. If this balance is upset, the flow of vital energy through the body, via the
energy channels or meridian lines, is blocked. These blockages
can be cleared by inserting acupuncture needles in the body at
certain points.

There are 12 main meridians. They are positioned symmetri-
cally, so that each one (and so the acupuncture points along it)
runs through both the left and right sides of the body.

As well as running along a superficial pathway just below the body surface, the meridians have a deep course through which they are connected to the inner organs. Three Yin and three Yang meridians begin, or end in the coronet region of each leg. These points on the coronet are called "Jing-well" points.

On the front side of the forelegs, above the toe, are the Jing-well points of the Yang meridians, while on the back side of the forelegs, above the heels, are the Jing-well points of the Yin meridians.

On the hind legs, the Jing-well points of the Yang meridians are located just above the toe and outer wall of the foot, and those of the Yin meridians above the inner wall and the heels and bulbs of the feet. In accordance with the divisions, or map, of the body surface and the course of the meridians, the muscles on the top and side of the head, neck, body and croup are designated as Yang muscles, and those underneath as Yin muscles. The front of the forelegs and the front and sides of the hind legs are Yang areas, and the back of the hind legs and the back and sides of the forelegs are Yin areas.

The extensor muscles are predominantly Yang, and most of the flexor muscles are Yin. It is inevitable that the imbalance in the feet, muscles and the way of going of a crooked horse will upset the balance of Yin and Yang and interfere with the balanced flow of energy through the meridians of each side.

Therapeutic aspects

It is obvious from the above description why acupuncture is so effective in the treatment and prevention of health-related problems.

However, to achieve lasting success in the treatment of a horse affected by a pronounced natural crookedness, we need to pay attention to every aspect, that is, everything that goes to make up this crookedness, which therefore needs to be taken into account in its treatment:

- Establishing physical and mental balance through the use of holistic medicine.
- Regular attention to the feet.
- Correction of the "wrong" way of going and "wrong" musculature through skilled training and schooling.

Dr. Med. Vet. Martina Steinmetz
Friedrich Ebert Strasse 45
D-68535 Edingen
Neckarhausen
Germany
martina-steinmetz@web.de

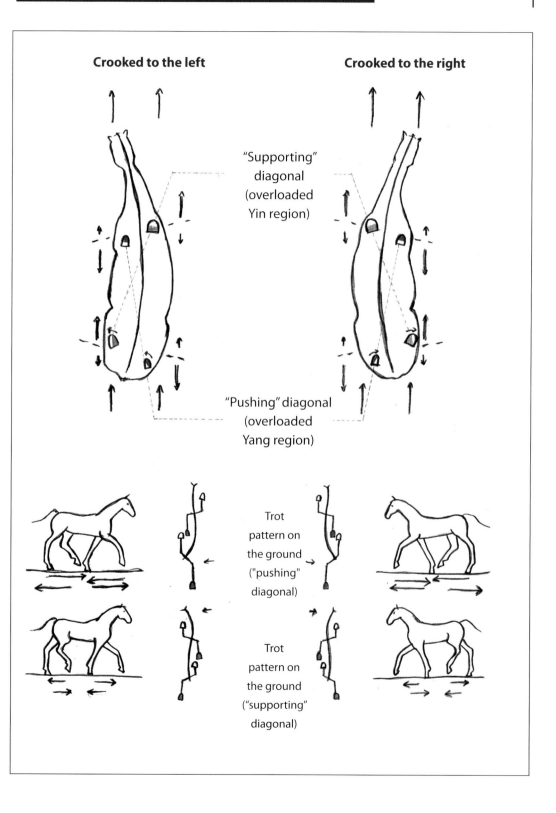

Crooked to the left

Crooked to the right

"Supporting" diagonal (overloaded Yin region)

"Pushing" diagonal (overloaded Yang region)

Trot pattern on the ground ("pushing" diagonal)

Trot pattern on the ground ("supporting" diagonal)

● A "horse-friendly" system of management! The horse should have plenty of opportunity for stimulation, exercise and moving "straight ahead," which means turnout, if possible, with other horses.

ANDREA LÜBKE-HAYER

Use of Bach Flower remedies in straightness training

Many of the horses that come to the *ARR*® Center for straightness training are no longer "in balance," either physically or mentally.

On the physical level, this imbalance upsets the way of going. This is because the weight is distributed wrongly, there is excess weight on certain limbs, and there are muscle tensions and restrictions, or "blocks," in the area around the withers. Constantly trying to compensate and keep its balance places the horse under stress.

The psychological stress then causes even more physical problems—not only in its way of going, but other kinds of health problems. To understand this we only have to look at the "psychosomatic" illnesses that are becoming increasingly common in humans.

We know, however, that psychological stress frequently causes problems in the way of going. For example, we know that young horses are often put under stress in training through rushing and rough-and-ready methods. It is impossible for these horses to work with freedom and looseness. In the long term, this constant tension results in problems in the muscles and the overall way of going.

Similarly, a horse that has had an accident or traumatic experience often tenses up and creates a lasting defensive "block," which will not usually disappear of its own accord. The way the horse is kept is also important for its mental well-being—the horse needs social contact, exercise and fresh air. If the system of management does not cater to the horse's biological and psychological needs (that is, allow it to "be a horse"), it will become stressed. The symptoms of this stress will differ greatly depending on the individual. Badly fitting, painful tack, dental problems, bad shoeing and a rider who sits crookedly, can also upset the horse, and cause it to be "out of balance."

With all these horses, Bach Flower remedies can be used as an aid in breaking down the "blocks," and help the horse to reestablish its mental and physical equilibrium. It is important that at the same time any training, tack and management problems are resolved. Even with these remedies, there can be no improvement, certainly in the long term, if the underlying causes remain.

It was at the beginning of the last century that Dr. Edward Bach developed his 38 "flower remedies." The subtle action of specially prepared plant essences helps animals (and people) to reestablish their mental harmony, come to terms with trauma, dispel their anxieties and develop self-confidence. Every animal or person needs his own individual "prescription" or mixture, and also sometimes his particular dosage.

Unlike synthetic medicinal drugs, the effect of Bach remedies is to bring about a return to mental balance and harmony. In other words, instead of suppressing the symptoms for a while, they allow the causes to be "broken down." In this way, the Bach remedies allow the horse's true nature to come to the fore: the horse can "be itself" again. It is important to realize, however, the remedies cannot be used to create new attributes to suit the owner or make the horse behave in a certain way. They serve only to bring out the horse's natural attributes and aptitudes. The horse is then able to live its life to the full and achieve its potential.

We have found from years of experience using Bach remedies as a complementary treatment to the straightness training that with many horses, it is a quick, stress-free method of getting them to accept the new training, give up old habits and fears, and so increase the success rate of the straightness training—or shorten the time required for it. These remedies are an important element in the integrated approach to solving the problem.

For the interested reader, there are many books available, in both the human and the veterinary sector, on the subject of Bach Flower remedies. These include some aimed specifically at horses and riders.

The rider frequently decides to undergo treatment with Bach remedies at the same time as the horse. This often works well

Andrea Lübke-Hayer
Naturheilpraxis für Pferde
und Kleintiere
(*Naturopathy Practice for Horses and Small Animals*)
Bahnhofstrasse 10
D-54518 Platten
Germany

because a problem in the rider's mind can have implications for the horse, especially when the horse's and rider's problems are connected.

Also, we must not underestimate the effects of the many unnatural environmental influences to which animals and people are subjected in this day and age, and the fact that many behavior problems are favored by selective breeding.

NOEL
M. DINJENS

The horse's teeth—that all important look inside the horse's mouth

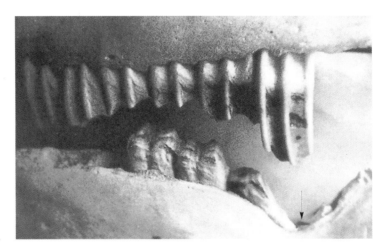

❙ Step mouth.

If we are to take a holistic approach to curing the horse's crookedness, we need to check and, if necessary, correct its teeth.

It is common to find deviations from the normal. When horses' teeth were examined at a major abattoir, about 80 percent of a total of 500 horses and foals were found to have irregularities in their mouths, ranging from sharp points and edges on the teeth (accompanied by damage to the mucous membrane lining the mouth), to "step-mouth" and "shear mouth."

In spite of the frequent occurrence of tooth problems, horse dentistry is a specialization that was long neglected in classical veterinary training. Although most veterinary practitioners stress that dental care is an integral part of the horse's training program, because of their heavy workload they have not had the time to acquire the necessary theoretical knowledge to use it in their everyday practice.

The following symptoms suggest tooth problems

- Head shaking

- Sensitivity around the head

- Problems cropping, picking up and chewing food

- Not eating

- Marked weight loss

- Temporomandibular joint (TMJ) problems

- Abscess in the mouth

- Digestive problems

- Physical changes

- Not accepting the bit

Since horses use their teeth to crop, pick up and chew their food, and since the gums and other parts of the mouth are richly supplied with blood and lymph vessels, as well as nerve channels, it is obvious that any irregularities in the teeth will have an adverse effect on the horse's health and well-being.

Until now, the effect of the horse's natural crookedness on the mouth and teeth had not been the subject of any detailed research.

The most common problems in adult horses are sharp points ("hooks") on the outside edges of the upper rear molars. These cause injury to the mucous membrane lining the mouth (see photo). Because of the pain this causes, the horse cannot chew, and so digest its food properly.

Irregularities in the teeth, and the consequences of these irregularities, seriously affect the horse's performance. Corrective or preventive treatment is therefore very important. The horse dentist or veterinarian who carries out this treatment has a selection of instruments at his disposal. He may use electric rasps and grinders, or a hand rasp, also known as a "float." Some practitioners prefer electric tools, others the traditional hand tools.

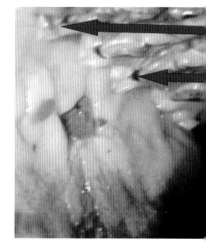

Injuries to the mucous membranes in the mouth.

Rasping by hand has big advantages

- The horse does not usually need to be sedated.
- Very little risk of damaging the tooth through overheating.
- The horse dentist or vet has more control over what he is doing.

When large pieces of tooth have to be removed, however, it is usually necessary to resort to an electric rasp.

How does the horse dentist operate?

First of all, he gains the confidence of the horse and the owner—one reassures the other! He washes the horse's mouth out with a disinfectant solution to get rid of remains of any food, and to enable him to make an accurate diagnosis.

He checks the movement of the lower jaw in relation to that of the upper jaw, runs his fingers over all the jaw, and checks the inside of the mouth for any irregularities in the teeth or mucous membrane. Injuries to the mucous membrane on the inside of the cheek are common near the sharp-edged teeth.

All incisors and cheek teeth are felt to make sure they are not loose or damaged.

Any wolf teeth are checked to see if they are sensitive, thus causing problems with the bit (wolf teeth are rudimentary extra premolars on the section of gum normally devoid of teeth that lies between the incisors and the cheek teeth).

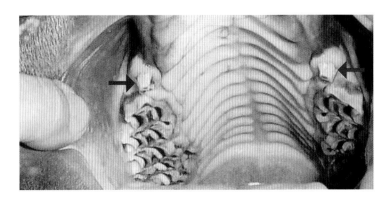

The wolf teeth can clearly be seen in this photograph.

Sometimes wolf teeth are present but have not erupted. These invisible or "blind" wolf teeth tend to cause the most problems. (As general practice, it is also a good idea for the rider to look in the horse's mouth from time to time to see if there are any problems with these teeth, or others.)

This preliminary examination gives the dentist or veterinary practitioner a general idea of the condition of the horse's mouth, and he then explains to the handler what needs to be done.

Normally, he begins by rasping the cheek teeth in the upper jaw. Since the rows of teeth in the upper jaw are further apart than those in the lower jaw, he can do this without a dental wedge gag or speculum. All he needs to do is push the rasp into the side of the mouth just inside the cheek. This is a good way to get the horse used to what is being done.

Then the horse is given a local anesthetic for the removal of any wolf teeth. While waiting for the anesthetic to take effect, the horse dentist will rasp the cheek teeth in the lower jaw, this time using a dental gag or speculum in the horse's mouth. It is important not to remove too much material from the chewing surface, which could prevent the teeth making contact with the teeth in the row above—damage the "bite." The wolf teeth are then removed, and the tushes may also be shortened.

Making a so-called "bit seat," by rounding the front edges of the first cheek teeth will ensure that the bit fits comfortably and can work properly.

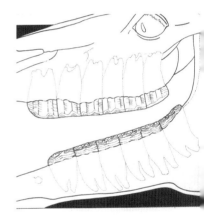

A "bit seat" has been created.

Once the dentist or vet is satisfied that all the pathological irregularities have been corrected, the horse's mouth is washed out to remove any remaining fragments of tooth.

As has already been mentioned, most of this kind of work can be done in the stall, box or stable area without sedation. For more serious problems, such as a broken tooth or root canal infection, the preferred course of action is to take the horse to a clinic, where it can be operated on under general anesthetic.

Noel M. Dinjens
Roosterbergstraat
B-303680 Maaseik
Belgium
noeldinjens@skynet.be

GERD LAMBERTY

The meaning of a "balanced foot"

A balanced foot is an important prerequisite for a successful performance horse.

To perform efficiently, a horse needs a sound, healthy foundation, which comprises of its feet.

Only if the foot is correctly aligned and symmetrical is it the right shape and sufficiently stable to carry weight properly and allow the horse's action and movement to be optimized. This is what is known as a "balanced foot."

When you look at the foot from the front, an imaginary line drawn down through the center of the cannon bone should divide the foot into two equal parts. Weight is then distributed evenly as the horse is working and the loading on the joints is symmetrical. This is known as the *mediolateral balance.*

Looked at from the side, the pastern and the foot should be in a straight line, that is, the "foot-pastern axis", or "toe axis" should be straight and unbroken. The front part of the wall (toe) should be parallel to the back of the wall (heel). This is known as the *dorsal-palmar balance.*

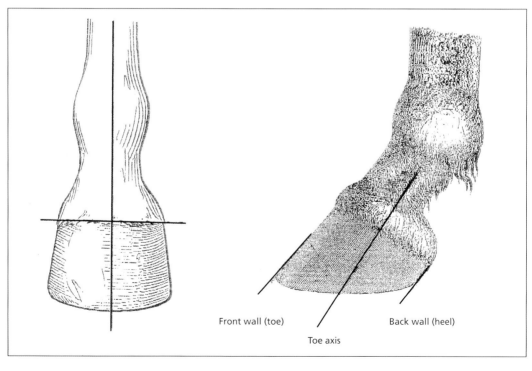

Front wall (toe)　　　　　Back wall (heel)

Toe axis

◐ *Mediolateral foot balance.*　　　　　◐ *Dorsal-palmar foot balance.*

If the foot is unbalanced or does not fully satisfy the requirements of a symmetrical, correctly aligned foot, the following problems can arise:

- Navicular disease
- Stumbling
- Cracks and splits in the wall of the foot
- Short strides
- Back problems

If these problems are to be avoided, attention must be paid to correct trimming and preparation of the foot.

When the correct balance has been restored, shoeing is not normally necessary. However, the quality of the horn and the surface on which the horse is worked are important considerations. If after the foot has been trimmed it is still not yet in balance, or the wear is excessive owing to adverse ground conditions, it is advisable to shoe the horse.

In this case, however, it is essential for the requirements to be discussed with owner, trainer and possibly the veterinary practitioner. The shoe must support the back of the foot especially, in the heel region.

To support the heel, the shoe needs to be long enough, and sufficiently wide in proportion to its length (see photos p. 138). This, in conjunction with a correct "toe axis," will enable the joints of the foot and lower leg to work at maximum efficiency.

However, correct shoeing alone is not enough. The horse needs to be capable of self-carriage. The farrier cannot succeed on his own: the horse's heaviness on the forehand and crookedness also need to be addressed. The reverse also applies: if the foot is not balanced, or is incorrectly trimmed or shod, the horse is not in a position to carry the weight efficiently. However hard he tries, the rider or trainer cannot achieve his aims if the foundations are not correct.

All those involved—the trainer, the rider, the veterinarian and farrier—need to pull together, and work toward the same goal. This is the only way to find a lasting solution to the problem.

We need to make a concerted effort to keep our horses sound for a good long time.

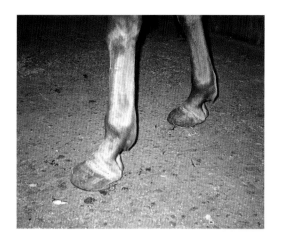

Before: Incorrect shoeing.

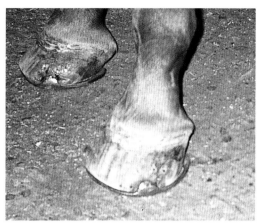

After: The balance of the foot has been restored.

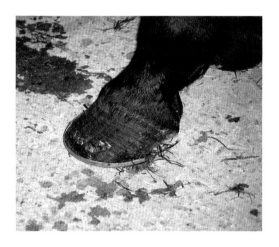

Before: Incorrect shoeing.

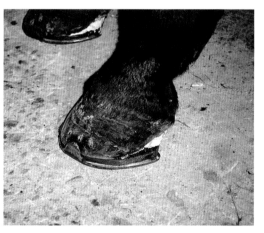

After: The balance of the foot has been restored.

Gerd Lamberty
Huf- and Beschlagschmied
(*Farrier*)
Am Plei 1
B-4730 Raeren
Belgium

The saddle: the connection between horse and rider

HANS SPIRIG

If we are to obtain optimum performance from a horse, we must do all we can to identify the causes of any problems. As saddlers, we too have had to study and concern ourselves with the horse's natural innate crookedness and its consequences, which are the subject of this book. We have then had to consider how much this should influence the way we fit a saddle.

When fitting a saddle we have to take into account the swinging of the back and the associated freedom of the shoulder and wither region. Only if these are allowed for will the horse be able to be comfortable.

For the best possible fit, the following points are especially important:

Front of the tree

The shape of the front arch of the tree should be such that the saddle sits behind the shoulder, and does not slip forward. It is important to preserve the freedom of the shoulders so as not to restrict the freedom of movement of the forehand. The arch also serves to prevent the saddle touching the horse's withers.

Center section

The middle section of the saddle's tree must not interfere with the upward swinging of the horse's back. If it is the wrong shape, it will place too much weight on certain parts of the horse's back and not distribute the rider's weight evenly.

Panels

The panels are the padded parts of the saddle that are in contact with the horse's back. It is important that at the back end of the saddle they do not press too hard on the horse, since this interferes with impulsion.

What should panels do?

They provide an even contact surface over the whole length of the saddle. They distribute the rider's weight evenly, and not concentrate the weight in specific areas.

When do panels cause problems?

First, when the padding is uneven or lumpy or the panels are overstuffed, and second, when they are stuffed with the wrong material, which can also cause unevenness.

Once the panels have been correctly stuffed, the padding should not be modified or added to. It should certainly be checked at intervals (which will depend on the amount of use) by an experienced saddler. It may be a good idea to re-flock the saddle from scratch if the stuffing has become so compacted that it seems hard and uneven, that is, worn out.

When deciding on the thickness of the stuffing, it is important to take the rider's weight into account. The back muscle can only work freely and without interference if the panels are in the best possible shape. Only then can the horse swing through its back and develop impulsion.

Girth

The girth is also important. The girth should hold the saddle on the horse in such a position that weight is evenly distributed over the back; it must not cause too much weight to be placed on the shoulders or any other part of the back.

Seat

From the rider's point of view, the most important aspects of a saddle are the seat and the position of its lowest point. For the rider's weight to remain as evenly distributed as possible on the horse's back, the lowest point of the seat must be in the center of the saddle. Only then can the rider sit in balance.

The rider must remain supple and "loose," so that he can swing with the horse. His position is therefore important. He must be able to sit in balance without "locking" his upper leg in position. A too narrow or too short seat restricts the rider and the swinging of the horse's back underneath him.

Riding in balance means sitting upright and straight. It also means the rider's seat is independent and supple, and does not interfere with the horse's movement. The rider seems to be "fused" with the horse's back.

Sometimes the rider is advised to adopt a set position that will ensure that he is in balance, but I cannot help wondering how he can then move with the horse. Also, when the horse swings through its back, it will have to cope with the strain of carrying the rider's weight as a fixed, rigid burden on it.

If the lowest point of the seat is toward the back of the saddle, the rider will adopt what is known as a "chair seat." This causes too much of the weight to be placed on the back of the saddle, and so on the part of the horse's back that lies under it. In the case of a "fork seat," on the other hand, there is too much weight on the front of the saddle, which causes pressure on the horse's shoulders, which restricts the freedom of movement of the forehand.

Knee rolls

The position of the knee rolls is as important as that of the lowest point of the seat. When the rider is sitting in an upright position, it should be possible to place a finger between the front of the thigh and the back of the knee roll. The knee rolls play a supporting role, helping the rider maintain a correct, supple seat. They should assist in energetic extended gaits, and in changes of balance. They help the rider to maintain a correct position but are not there to keep the rider in one set position. If the rider has to rely on the knee rolls to maintain his position, then the lowest point of the seat of the saddle is too far back or too far forward, or the rider is not sitting correctly.

Hans Spirig
Sattlermeister (*Saddler*)
Spirig Pferdesport St.Gallen
CH-9000 St.Gallen
Switzerland

DORIS SCHWAB, PROFESSIONAL RIDER

My first encounter with the trainers from the *Zentrum für ARR®* was in Avanches, in Switzerland. Along with my friend Peter Brechbül, I attended various courses about *Schiefen-Therapie®*, and found them very interesting.

The first course began with a presentation of the problems that can be caused by crookedness. These explanations, by Klaus Schöneich, aroused my curiosity. I was at the same time both shocked and fascinated. My head was buzzing. At the end of the course I knew that I had to take this further!

The best way to do this was obviously to go to the Center itself. So we took it in turns to drive to Germany with horses that we were training.

The Center, at that time in Rheurdt (it is now in Bedburg-Hau), was surrounded by fields, and there was a lovely peaceful atmosphere--very beneficial for both horse and rider.

The horses that go to the Center for corrective training spend half the day in the field, and are worked every day by Klaus Schöneich or Gabriele Schöneich-Rachen.

After three to six weeks—depending on the horse's progress —the rider becomes involved in the training. First, he is taught how to longe the horse. Then, the work on the rider's seat and the ridden work begin. Horse and rider are allowed to go home when they have reached a satisfactory level of understanding.

When a new horse arrives, a video recording is made of it being longed to enable a diagnosis to be made. The next stage is to devise a plan of action, which includes a saddle-fitting session, an appointment with the farrier, and if necessary treatment by a homeopath.

It was especially interesting for me to watch the new arrivals impartially. At first, they were irregular, that is, they displayed rhythm faults. Often, they were not well muscled, were completely devoid of impulsion, and their coats and eyes were dull. I then saw them change rapidly and almost beyond recognition.

I myself had to go through the *Schiefen-Therapie®* training process. I must say that I enjoyed each element of the training immensely. The emphasis was on freeing-up the horse's shoulders and getting it in balance.

After a week of preparation on the longe, I could ride my horses with just my seat, without spurs and without using my legs.

It felt wonderful. The horses lifted their backs and worked in response to just my seat aids. They went calmly, were "round" and in balance, and worked through their backs with freedom and looseness. It was everything I had dreamed of.

It sounds simple, but it is certainly not so. However, this system, which entails working the horse on the longe, *can* be learned.

Just as the horse was originally taught to respond to the leg and spurs, it must now learn to respond to the rider's seat and hips. If a horse can feel a fly on its skin, it must be possible to train it to be highly responsive to seat and hip aids.

I rode many horses each day, and unlike before, I was almost as fresh in the evening as when I started work in the morning. The hardest thing for me was changing my way of thinking and maintaining concentration. I had to concentrate on feeling what was going on underneath me while I was riding. My attention was drawn to things that I had experienced before, but not understood. These "details" are often very important to the corrective training.

One most important thing that I had to learn was how devastating the consequences would be if I reverted to my old style of riding.

I am often asked if I intend to ride like this all the time, including in competition. The answer to this is quite simple: this is not a new way to ride. The rider rides in this way in order to make the horse straight and to balance it. Once the horse is working freely through its back, it can be ridden normally, though with the lightest of aids.

It is most important also that the rider knows if his horse is right-handed or left-handed (whether the right or left forefoot is dominant).

Of course, a good trainer will see if the horse is falling onto its shoulder in the half-pass, as an example. However, if in its preparatory work and in the "loosening" phase, the horse is longed and ridden in accordance with the Schöneichs' system, these mistakes should no longer happen. The horse also stands a better chance of learning the more advanced exercises, and in a way that it will not forget them.

If you watch a video in slow motion of a horse that is crooked and on the forehand, you realize when you see it trotting a circle how much strain there must be on the tendons, ligaments, knees and shoulders. Horses that are in balance need far less attention from the veterinarian!

Most of the problems begin when the horse is first started. You are told that young horses should always be ridden forward and downward. This is absolutely right. But for you to be able to do so, the horse's crookedness first needs to be corrected, and in my opinion, almost the only way to do this successfully is through the straightness training longe work described in this book.

Every rider and trainer should try moving on all fours. He will then have a better understanding of the problems we are making for the horse when we ride it. Obviously the more that is expected of the horse in terms of performance, the greater the problem.

Let's be absolutely honest: how often do we see rhythm faults, for example in international dressage competitions? We have the means to change and improve all this!

I advise you to study this book carefully, and to think about the methods you are using. This system of straightness training (or anti-crookedness training) should be seen as a small revolution in horse training. It provides the answer to many problems. As a trainer of many years' experience, I can recommend it to you wholeheartedly.

Doris Schwab
Ausbildungsstall
(*Training Stable*)
Hauptstrasse 98
CH-1794 Salvenach
Switzerland

Six Testimonials

ELISABETH
EVERSFIELD

In May 2003, I bought a state-approved PRE (Spanish) stallion in Madrid. He didn't settle in at all well. He was very withdrawn with people, and the slightest thing stressed him. At the beginning, we did not notice any particular problems when riding him. However, he gradually became more and more tense and hurried in his way of going, sometimes to the point of panicking.

We cut down his training and called in a horse physiotherapist.

In October, we found the horse trembling and bathed in sweat in his stall. It took a long time to calm him down, and after that he kept having panic attacks. His condition grew visibly worse, so we took him to the university clinic in Giessen. He was given a complete examination, and no explanation was found. After two weeks at the clinic he was sent back home. About two weeks later he started shaking again. He was soaked in sweat and running round his box in a panic. This time it was so bad that the veterinarian thought there was very little hope for him. The horse was taken back to the university clinic in Giessen. Again, nothing was found. Since I wanted to establish whether the horse could still be ridden, we were sent to the university clinic in Munich for an MRI (magnetic resonance imaging) scan. He was finally released four weeks later. Nothing had shown up on the MRI scan either. However, the long-term prognosis was that it was unlikely he could continue to be used as a riding or competition horse. In the meantime, I was just thankful that he was still alive, and was prepared to keep him and let him live out his days in the paddock.

By sheer chance, an acquaintance had mentioned the *Zentrum für ARR®* in Rheurdt. An appointment was quickly arranged for the problem to be assessed. At Rheurdt, the horse was first of all longed in a cavesson and at the same time filmed with a camcorder. Then his problems were discussed and analyzed, and it was ascertained whether he was right-handed or left-handed, which was important later for the way we rode him on each rein. Klaus Schöneich cheered me up when he was sure he could turn the horse around. The horse then stayed on for three weeks of corrective training. I was asked to attend during the last week.

I was delighted when I saw my horse again. He was absolutely "radiant" and clearly enjoying life again. For the first two days there, I was faced with longeing. It was not easy, but I wanted to learn this system. Klaus Schöneich patiently explained to me over and over again what it was all about: the essence being that the horse must be in balance—it must be able to carry itself before it can carry a rider!

Back home again, I was once more on my own. I stuck resolutely to the instructions I had been given. Gradually, when I was riding, I began to see small glimmers of light at the end of the tunnel. And then, I suddenly noticed that the horses (I had gone over to using this system with all of my horses) were moving with ever-increasing lightness. I no longer needed to apply any pressure, or use any auxiliary aids. I had finally discovered what I had always been trying to achieve. In the meantime, I have introduced all my pupils to the Schöneich system, with the same positive results.

Personally, I am very pleased that I took this step, and can only encourage everybody considering this route not to allow themselves to be put off, but simply to go ahead and do it. They will not be disappointed! Since then, my horse has been placed three times among the first five in Medium level dressage tests. He will shortly be taking part in his first Advanced level test.

The first time we took horses to the *Zentrum für ARR®* for training was in 1995. We were there with our horses (a Fjord gelding and a Barb mare) for just two weeks. We were amazed, right at the beginning, that after running his hands over the horses and longeing them, Klaus Schöneich was able to describe the problems we were encountering when we rode them. He was absolutely "spot-on" with his remarks. A lot of the things that were explained to us were different from what we had been taught by our previous trainers. But the nice thing about it was that all was explained until we understood it; we learned that everything is interconnected, and why certain problems arise when we are riding. We observed everything with a very critical eye and tested it out, and compared it to what we had been taught before. Finally, we were convinced that this really was the better way. On previous courses we had been on, we had always taken everything in and felt very motivated, but four weeks later if we asked ourselves what we had gained from

BIRGIT
BACHER

it, we found everything had reverted to how it was before the course. This was different after our stay in Rheurdt: since we had to start again almost from scratch, we first had to take a step backward. However, we then started to move forward, with confidence. We decided at this point to go to the Center for all our future riding training, so we are now regular visitors. Over the years, we have taken all our horses there for training: our Barb gelding Sirhan, our Barb mares Kahida and Yagmur, and our Barb stallion Vharib. Vharib was taken to the Center at the age of two-and-a-half years for a month's training on the longe. The aim was to make him straight.

He was then backed at three-and-three-quarter years. At five years old, after further training, he was due to be put forward for grading. He was a top class horse, he looked good and moved well, only the rider—myself, that is—needed to be brought up to scratch. We had a full week at the Center before the stallion grading in which to train, and we made intensive use of the time. Everyone went to a lot of trouble to help and support Vharib and me. Small adjustments were made to the aids, and the bit was changed because Vharib was just getting his stallion teeth (tushes) and was having trouble with the snaffle. We practiced riding in company. Finally Klaus Schöneich said that I should make sure I did not "disturb" Vharib, and he would then do very well.

In spite of me being very nervous, Vharib was graded with a Class 1 Premium, was Champion Graded stallion, Champion Barb Breeding Stallion and Best of Show. As well as his outstanding breed "type" and conformation, he received a high score for his action. His uphill canter, in particular, was highly commended.

At the *Berbertreffen 2002* (2002 Barb horse breed show), he was again Champion Barb Breeding Stallion. The judges' comment: "Outstanding breed type and presence, dynamic forward/upward trot with a well-defined rhythm." In December 2002, at the international championship in Paris organized by the *Europäischer Berberverband* (European Barb Association), Vharib was Champion Breeding Stallion, and Supreme Champion.

We are convinced that the high scores he achieved for his action were largely due to the anatomically correct training he had received.

All in all we are very satisfied, even though sometimes things do not go to according to plan. Horses are not machines, and we as riders cannot always get everything right.

I had owned El Shakhi, my purebred Arabian for a good two years when he fell one day and hurt his left knee quite badly. The wound had only just healed when he fell once more, opening it up again. This time it happened during a "handy horse" competition.

Then, two months later, he cut it open again on the fence in the field and had to go to the animal hospital, where he spent more than two months on complete stall rest. It was at this point that I began to wonder what was causing the problems.

All the veterinarians I consulted told me I would never be able to ride my horse again. Then, after a long search, I managed to get help from the team at the *ARR*®.

I had met Klaus Schöneich at a course held at the *NPZ* (national horse center) in Bern, Switzerland. His method appealed to me immediately. I liked the caring, respectful way in which he handled each horse. Having listened to my tale of woe, he took all Shakhi's X-rays back to the Center with him, where everything was analyzed by his team of experts.

It turned out that the main cause of the falls was the horse's hitherto undiagnosed crookedness and his extreme heaviness in front, both of which had been made worse by incorrect training. I was told that these two problems have far-reaching consequences, and need to be corrected in every horse's training. This was all new to me.

Unfortunately, an understanding of the classical training upon which this is based, is fast disappearing. We live in an age where rapid results are more important. People do not allow enough time to lay down a solid foundation, either in their own or their horse's training.

However, sooner or later they have to pay the price, and this can be high in both emotional and financial terms.

We were lucky: contrary to veterinary opinion, we were able to make Shakhi rideable again and enable him to enjoy his work once more. As his owner and now also his trainer, I learned to train him correctly and in a way that was right for him, both on the longe and under saddle.

FABIENNE KÄNEL

◗ *Fabienne Känel with Shakhi.*

Renata van Känel with Solero.

RENATA
VAN KÄNEL

When my PRE (Spanish) horse Solero was declared incurable after veterinary investigations revealed arthrosis and kissing spines, I was told that it would be better to put him out to grass and not ride him anymore, or to ride him only slowly, in walk. And he wasn't the easiest horse to manage in the field or the stable. My whole world had collapsed. When I had bought Solero a few years previously in Spain, he was as sound as a bell, and had been properly trained. Now, so soon afterward, he had been condemned to death.

When the vets did not know what to do except give him cortisone injections, I felt it would be better to send my horse, who had once been so full of life, to that "stable in the sky" rather than cause him further suffering through pain and loss of movement.

Then, through a colleague, I met Fabienne Känel. It was almost as if she had been sent to help me. Solero was indeed too young to die and, in the meantime, I have found out what was wrong with him. After a two-month stay at *ARR*®, his muscles have all built up again, so his arthrosis and kissing spines condition are not causing him any trouble. I, too, received two weeks of intensive training and was able to continue the horse's training at home without difficulty. If I had any questions, Gabriele Rachen-Schöneich or Klaus Schöneich would give me follow-up advice by telephone, or Fabienne would come round —the problems with our horses had brought us together, and she was now an irreplaceable and valued friend.

As a result of his correct gymnastic training, Solero now spontaneously starts to perform more advanced exercises, such as passage, of his own accord and without any input from me. I shall never again have to use excessive leg pressure or ride him with spurs. He now goes forward happily again—even some-times a bit too enthusiastically—in response to the lightest of aids. I get angry when I think what many horses go through when they are being ridden, and all because the rider, and also the trainer, will not admit to their own lack of skill. I consider that the corrective training work at *ARR* ® not only enables the horse to achieve its potential, but also helps the rider to prog-ress and develop.

BEATE MOLL

Calando, my seven-year-old Rheinland gelding, snorts content-edly and is immersed in his work. During our warm-up phase, we have no concerns about the other four horses and riders in our 20 x 60 meter indoor school, even though they are having a jumping lesson. Neither are we bothered by the sound of fall-ing poles. My horse goes as if of his own accord to the other end of the school so that I can put his sweat sheet (sweat rug) on and walk him round to dry him off. It doesn't bother him that there are children playing behind the wall. A friend comes up on her horse and asks me to take the lead with my quiet horse to help her mare to settle.

My horse is relaxed as he walks to the longe ring, and not at all concerned that we have to go past a dark corner. While I am longeing, the tractors are busy outside, the farm truck clatters past the ring, the giant-sized tractor has to be moved—and all this less than 20 meters away. Calando is concentrating on my body language and working willingly on the circle. All this sounds very harmonious and idyllic, but it was not always like that.

It was love at first sight. I bought Calando when he was five years old. He had just been broken. However, shortly after arriving at our yard, the saga began. He became panicky, tense and extremely nervous. The slightest thing caused him to panic and he soon became uncontrollable, both to ride and to lead. He was treated by an osteopath, his diet was changed, and a veterinarian was consulted, but to no avail. We tried everything! At first, we proceeded very patiently, then we put the pressure on and tried a more energetic approach, then finally we even resorted to force. But the horse's behavior became more and more extreme. If he was worked for two days in a row he bucked and reared and did everything he could to get rid of the hated rider. Something was wrong with him. In the meantime, I had asked everyone I could think of for help.

I had run out of ideas. After coming off him for the umpteenth time, I was on the verge of giving him, or selling him very cheaply, back to the breeder. By now I was terrified of riding him. When led, he could only be controlled in the part of the arena nearest the door. The turning point was a trip to EQUITANA 2003. I visited the *ARR®* stand and my attention was drawn to a video of a horse that was behaving exactly the same as my horse. Everything that Gabriele Rachen-Schöneich and Klaus Schöneich were saying about their corrective training for crookedness, their *Schiefen-Therapie®*, made sense and sounded very simple. They described my horse's behavior to me down to the last detail.

At the beginning of March 2003, I set off with Calando for Rheurdt. First, a precise diagnosis was made. Calando was assessed—first standing still and finally in trot on the longe—by the veterinarian Tina Rasch, the farrier Huub Geerst, and the Schöneichs. In the discussion that followed, a video recording of Calando in movement was used to show exactly where his problems lay. Because of his natural inborn crookedness—he was extremely right-handed—he could not lift his right foreleg properly. Of course, he had to use his whole body to compensate for this and try to keep his balance. As a result, he was very much on the forehand, he turned his knees outward slightly, and was irregular in his gaits. On top of this, his feet had been badly trimmed and were crooked, and the muscles on the underside of his neck were overdeveloped while his back muscles were underdeveloped. I quickly realized from these images that for all these months the pain and discomfort had simply been driving the horse mad. I think the worst thing about it was that he had never been able to escape the tension.

Yet all this was about to change! After a week at the *ARR*® Center, Calando was almost unrecognizable. He went willingly on the longe in the round pen, concentrating and responding to Klaus Schöneich's body language. All traces of panic had disappeared. His musculature had changed visibly and he was much more regular in his gaits. I was very encouraged because it meant there was a chance for us after all. Under Klaus Schöneich's direction, I learned to longe my horse with a cavesson. I learned to interpret Calando's body language, and to communicate with him in a way he understood. We had finally found a common language.

We had made a start. Now there had to be a radical change in my behavior—and I had to learn to behave quietly and calmly with my horse and avoid raising my voice and reacting sometimes in a way that frightened him.

In the next phase, I had to get to know my horse from the saddle now that he had been completely transformed. It took some doing for me to come to terms with the idea of sitting on my formerly unpredictable horse with no reins. I mounted with shaking knees. It was wonderful! Calando was focused, full of impulsion and willing: the complete opposite of how he had been before. When we began working on my seat on the longe in the round pen, it became apparent that I was collapsing my left hip, which was putting my weight on the horse's right shoulder. This was making it even harder for the horse to lift his right foreleg. I had some lessons with Gabriele in which she corrected my seat. The better I sat, the more my horse relaxed and the more freely he moved. I had to learn to interpret signals from the horse—his body language—from the saddle as well as from the ground. I got better at this from one day to the next.

Then I started having lessons in the big outdoor arena instead of the round pen. Of course, here there were exciting things for Calando to see, and of course, he was occasionally frightened, but never again did he panic. I learned to work to correct my horse's crookedness and heaviness on the forehand. These lessons took place with the senior *Schiefen-Therapie®* trainers, and were conducted very calmly and patiently. The use of force was never, ever involved. An integrated approach was taken to our problems: Calando's body, feet, mind and way of moving were all assessed, as were his saddle, the fitting of the saddle, my seat, and how I behaved with the horse. My dealings with Calando were considered from every angle, and then as a whole.

Sometimes it feels as if I have been introduced by the *ARR®* team to color television. Most other riders seem to be watching television in black and white! It is very difficult to explain what colors are to someone who has never seen them. Calando and I are still in the early stages, and so far we are only acquainted with the primary colors, but we are very curious about the others.

Since my horse has become rideable again, thanks to the training he received at the Center, I go back regularly to make further progress along this road of discovery.

DANIELA BAYERL

Every time I go to the Center, I am struck by the way horses seem to move "on crutches" to start with, and then turn into athletic dancers. The owners are amazed, and often the new, unaccustomed impulsion causes them problems. Then, all of a sudden, they realize what a nice horse they have, and that they need to be able to sit on it properly and ride it sensitively.

These observations are interesting. Modern Warmblood breeding produces the perfect riding horse with a lot of action and talent, and powerful, active hindquarters. But how many perfect riders are there? What is the use of producing highly bred horses with outstanding gaits when hardly anyone can ride them properly?

These talented horses seem to tax the skills even of instructors and trainers—almost all of the owners had gone to a professional for help and advice on their problems before their horses were finally "cured" through straightness training. So are we breeding horses for a few gifted riders and neglecting the wider market?

Dressage is supposed to have the effect of building up the horse's musculature. Training should never cause the horse to *lose* muscle.

This could almost be considered one of the principles of training, since it is relevant to about 90 percent of the horses that come here. A young, unbroken horse comes equipped with everything necessary for a sound, healthy future. It is the rider who generates the problems. Frequently, because of his stubbornness and inflexibility, he will not use his common sense to find a solution. Moreover, his problems provide an opportunity for those trainers who promise rapid results. No wonder that many horse owners, working on their own, are tempted by these promises. Not knowing the correct way, they will clutch at any straw. To go back to the opening sentence above: the musculature is developed not through veterinary or any other treatment, but through correct, hard work. However, this work needs to be based on proper understanding.

Our success rate at the Center is very high—around 90 to 95 percent. This is not boasting: it is a fact. Of course, there are drawbacks to quoting statistics since lasting success depends on how good the rider is at sticking to the training afterward. Often, he finds it difficult when he returns to his original situation with its own problems. He has learned to do lots of things differently, and is confident that he has found a way to help prevent himself and his horse going back to their old ways. Unfortunately though, he will have to contend with doubters and cynics because he has left the well-trodden paths. He will need to ignore the criticism and simply get on with riding his horse.

Imagine a road—or a path—that has become impassable and needs to be repaired. So that the work can be done faster and more safely, a diversion is put in place. The diversion should always lead back to the original road. Diversions are normal and no-one gets excited about them. But, a rider may have problems trying to explain to an instructor that he needs to make a diversion, and that it is with this that he needs help. The success rate quoted above is further eroded by narrow-mindedness, rigid "sticking to the rules," and reluctance to look for solutions (which could also mean taking a long hard look at one's own faults).

IN CONCLUSION

Exercising control over the shoulders as a means of straightening the horse, as we recommend it, is not something we have discovered, but was part and parcel of the classical training of yesteryear. Yet not even this seems to help convince people that it is right. However, we should also mention that more and more trainers, as well as veterinary practitioners, are turning to our system and can see that it provides solutions.

Another piece of advice for our critics: before passing judgment, they should ask themselves why we are doing things in the way we are, and what we are trying to achieve. It is also important to ensure that what they have seen and are criticizing accurately represents our training methods. We are then happy to confront this criticism provided we also have the opportunity to compare our work with that of our detractor, and also pass comment on his system. This is the only way to sort things out.

One last word: many riders would like us to set out a step-by-step list of instructions, a sort of "recipe" for success along the lines of, "Take this, do that…" However, horses are all so different, and the influences of breeding, upbringing, handling and training are so strong that in the corrective training process that there can be no hard and fast rules. Any book such as this one can only serve to give an idea of what we do, which we have done to our best ability.